AF522616

TELEVISION AND EDUCATION

TELEVISION AND EDUCATION

By

Dr. Meenu Dev
M.A. (English) M.Ed, Ph.D. (Education)
Assistant Professor
Department of Education
MANUU, Hyderabad
(India)

DISCOVERY PUBLISHING HOUSE PVT. LTD.
NEW DELHI-110 002

Published by:
Namit Wasan
DISCOVERY PUBLISHING HOUSE PVT. LTD.
4383/4B, Ansari Road, Darya Ganj
New Delhi-110 002 (India)
Phone : +91-11-23279245, 43596064-65
Fax : +91-11-23253475
E-mail : discoverypublishinghouse@gmail.com
namitwasan9@gmail.com
sales@discoverypublishinggroup.com
web : www.discoverypublishinggroup.com

***First Edition:* 2018**

ISBN: 978-93-86841-28-5

Television and Education

Printed at:
Infinity Imaging Systems
Delhi

Preface

If you want to be somebody, Grow so says the great German philosopher, Goethe, as the golden prescription for education at all level of schooling, the basic aim of education being to help every individual grow to the optimum of one's potentials. The present work is an attempt to assess the effectiveness of educational television programme for improving primary education. The study entitled 'Television and Education' aims at improving the strategies of implementation of educational television programmes to meet the real need of the target group to improve the quality of primary education. The analysis and interpretation of the study has been made systematically to reflect the efficacy of television to improve the quality of primary schooling and accelerating achievement of children. An attempt has been made to collect qualitative data through survey and experimental method focus on teachers, third and fifth class children. Findings of the present study will be useful for improving and planning the instructional strategies for improving the teaching learning process.

The purpose of this book is to enrich the primary schooling.

It aims at improving the quality of primary schooling in the country. I am confident that professionals, practitioners, researchers will find this book quite informative and useful in planning, designing and implementing educational television programme to meet the needs of primary quality education.

I am highly grateful to Prof. L.C. Singh his constant support and guidance.

I specially thanks to Dr. Dhaiya, Director of SCERT Chandigarh, Dr. Sudarshan Mishra, RCU; Dr. Arun Kumar IGNTU for their valuable contributions in the form of brief snippets, clippings.

I also thank Dr. D.N. Khosla for pruning the text and making it praiseworthy through going inputs to shape it the way it is being presented as an academic – cum-research document to understand the leit motif of this piece of work and enjoy going through it as an humble attempt to boost for all and the children of different abilities.

The work is the outcome of the blessings and affections of my parents and all family members, who were always the source of my inspiration, motivation and success.

Dr. Meenu Dev

Contents

Preface

1. Introduction 1-5
2. Television and Education 6-13
3. Major Educational Television Projects 14-19
4. Role of Television for Globalization of Education 20-22
5. Television and wide Range of Instruction Strategies 23-27
6. Literature Related to Educational Television 28-61
7. Experimental Study on Educational Television Programme in India on South Zone Delhi Primary Schools 62-75
8. Analysis and Interpretation 76-105
9. Findings, Implications and Recommendations 106-120

Bibliography 121-131

Index 133-136

Introduction

Television has established itself as a medium of information, education and entertainment throughout the world (UNESCO, 1964). It is one of the most significant technological developments for rapid expansion of education. The educational use of television not only encourages the pupils but demands a continuous appraisal of the ways in which it is or it may be utilized. Kinder (1959) observes: "Television has literally captured the country. Its expansion has been much more dramatic than that radio or the automobile. It has become an important part of our way of life, so much so that it is difficult to say whether it is a luxury or a necessary" (p. 19)

Education is the most important single factor in achieving rapid economic development and for crating a democratic social order. The mass media of education, especially radio and television are powerful tools to provide qualitative instruction and for quantitative expansion of education at all levels. Emery, *et.al.* (1966) have rightly pointed out:

> "Television and radio are electronic magic carpets that transport millions of persons each day to far away places. They are the twentieth century creations of the technological revolution that has been transforming much of the world for almost two centuries and their impact on our social, political and cultural life has been profound".

Television programmes are more effective than radio programmes. Unlike the radio broadcast where only the sound is transmitted, television transmission has the added advantage of the all important visual experience which is made more dynamic and meaningful by the movement and sound associated with the visual experience. There are some complicated experiments which can be shown to many students or a large audience at a time by this audio-visual device. The techniques such as close-up and microscopic pictures can make the situation clearer and interesting. The use of television in education has grown sharply in recent years. Moreover, Education does not stop at the borders of the campus and television offers another way to reach out into homes and serve people where they live. (Emery, 1951).

Brown, *et.al.* (1964) have given the following special advantages of television:

1. It is a convenient and economical means of reaching enormous cross-sections of the population with simultaneous presentation.
2. It combines the best elements of radio (going right into the home or classroom with the potency of motion pictures.
3. It is capable of helping to overcome learning barriers for many persons presenting important ideas, helping to mould attitudes, providing information in ways which demand neither high verbal proficiency nor physical presence at the scene of action.
4. It is a means of multiplying "personal" contacts for outstanding TV instructors with students and adults all over the country or the world.
5. It is capable of helping to bring about needed social improvement and developments.
6. It capitalizes upon immediacy, upon the "here and now" aspects of communication.

Television is a very sophisticated medium of communication with unique qualities and capabilities for influencing education. It is a varitile and dynamic audio-visual device, which broadens the intellectual horizon of both the teachers and the taughts from time to time. The proper use of television provides new incentives for students to assume more responsibility for learning. It is also a fact effective television teaching demands more preparation and the assistance of more specialized personal than does conventional instruction television is not a self-contained education entity, but an instrument which is significantly only in the particular educational situation in which it is employed. It provides new and better ways of relating the activities of pupils, teachers and parents and demands a continuous appraisal of the way in which it is or may be utilized.

Influence of Television on Children

When one is aware of the extent to which an infant's first thoughts are conditioned by visual and auditory perceptions, it is easy to understand how powerful children are influenced by television. Concept learning and development of cognitive patterns in childhood are not solely the consequences of heredity: they owe much to the richness of the content in which meaning processes evolve. The experience of television plays a decisive role in defining this context.

Children's perceptive experiences of television and the process whereby they understand television message, are very closely related to their stage of development and to the syntaefical elements of audio-visual language. The size of the toys in advertisements provides a good example for this.

Television points up the unsolved societal/educational problems of reconciling technological innovations, political democracy, economic monopolies, foreign competition and a panorama of unmeant educational needs. Heavy viewing seems to bring children evaluated as having excellent English language skills (writing, reading and speaking).

Educational television has the potentiality of creating interest and motivation in both children and adults. It also facilitates training of teacher as the student-teacher or any other teacher observes good teachers in action and imitates various aspects of teaching and teaching skills. It has already proved its effectiveness and supremacy in teaching certain subjects. Koul (1987) has given some major prospects of educational television which are as follows:

- **Social Equality in Education:** Television promotes the goal of social equality in education catering to the masses of rural background and those living in slums or urban areas. Television increases the effectiveness of instruction and cuts down drop-out rates.
- **Higher Quality of Instruction:** Television programmes are well planned/organized and better presented than the visual classroom instruction.
- **Reduce Dependency on Teacher:** The students learn from television with their own efforts. They need minimum help from the teacher in case television is pressed into service.
- **Flexibility:** Rapid and continuing changes in curriculum and instructional methods are made possible through educational television. Courses can be constantly modified not only to update them but to incorporate the constantly changing needs of the society and the expansion of knowledge.
- **Mass Education:** Educational television can cater to the explosive increases in student numbers.

The purpose and objectives of educational television programmes are apparent. Besides the programmes for children, ETV pays emphasis on teacher education. In the words of Arve (1976):

> "The main objective of ETV project is to produce more schooling and better schooling, primarily for children. Teachers are also trained by ETV in many of the projects,

> but this is a part of the objective of reaching children. ETV is used to achieve these objectives because it is believed in the long run to be cheaper than traditional teaching".

Therefore, TV is a multi-media equipment by which different kinds of mass media and material can be utilized for producing and utilizing its programmes. In the advanced countries, it has remarkably influenced the life styles and education of the people. The real education of today cannot be made effective as well as efficient for the citizens of tomorrow without the support of this sophisticated instrument - Television.

The role of media and educational technology in the new system of education has been clearly defined in the 'National Policy on Education (1986/92). It has recommended as follows:

> "Modern communication technologies have the potential to bypass several stages and sequences in the process of development encountered in earlier decades. Both the constraints of time and distance at once becomes manageable. In order to avoid structural dualism, modern educational technology must reach out to the most distant areas and the most deprived sections of beneficiaries simultaneously with the areas of comparative affluence and ready availability" ...

> "The media have a profound influence on the minds of children as well as adults; some of them tend to be encourage consumerism, violence, etc., and have a deleterious effect. Radio and TV programmes which clearly militate against proper educational objectives will be prevented. Steps will taken to discourage such trends in films and other media also. An active movement will be started to provide the production of children's programme of high quality and usefulness".

2

Television and Education

Television is a channel for conveying whatever is put into it. Instructional television or television designed for direct use in the classroom must depend importantly upon classroom teacher audience for determination of its content, presentation and effective utilization. But while instructional television may change some of the things the classroom teacher does, the major change will be in the direction of training a teacher more productive use of his time rather than restricting him. It is clear that there are some teaching acts it can do superlatively with. It can let a large number of students look into a microscope at the same time. It can let a class watch and activity that would be spoiled by direct observation. It can share teaching and grant demonstrations.

There are some ways of using television which make far better learning than others. Experience indicates that most effective uses of television have been in situation where it has been combined carefully with other activities in a total learning situation; and where students were strongly motivated to learn from it. So the teacher who has devices work for him may not have exactly the same duties as before, but his duties become more exponential and the student who has devices working for him will spend his day exactly as before, but his learning opportunities will be considerably more.

The well planned television program can motivate students, guide and sharpen their reading by providing background and demonstrations, encourage responsibility for independent learning, arouse curiosity and develop new insights and the excitement of discovery.

Television as a means to improve the quality of instruction despite the teacher shortage: Television is an important means to improve the quality of instruction. It can be improved among other innovation to use television "as an integral part of the regular instructional programme" to help teacher and building shortages and at the same to improve the quality of education. It is a large dose of very human intelligence that needs proper guidance.

So television is a perfect example of how technology, by itself, cannot cultivate or improve human learning, nor human nature.

Television is a primary means of involving most of our nation in the humanities today. In education, television must impressive use in extending the range of a gifted teacher beyond a single classroom. Whether a broadcast system is available to pupils in many schools may be taught simultaneously by a particularly able teacher prior to a more personal instructor and discussion of the subject matter in individual classes with local teacher in attendance.

History of Educational Television

Beginning in the USA

In 1932, a small cluster of people on a Midwestern University Campus witnessed what was probably the first educational T.V. Programme to be telecast anywhere. They were presented over waXK and experimental station developed by the state university of Iowa Electrical Engineering Department. Using a "scanning disc" system, instead of a picture tube, the station transmitted more than 400 programmes including lecture courses in art, shorthand, engineering and botany, as well as Drama and other entertainment between 1932 and 1939.

The year 1948 found five U.S. educational institutions seriously involved with television and television planning. The State University of Iowa had applied to be Federal Communication Commission (FCC) for permission to construct a station. Its sister institution Iowa State College (now Iowa State University) had received a construction permit from the FCC. Kansas State College was operating as experimental station on channel I (since removed from the broadcast band by the FCC). The University of Michigan and American University in Washington, D.C., equipped with studies of their own, were producing programmes for broadcast over commercial television station transmitters and other new developments where underway. In February, 1950 WOI TV at IOWA State College began regular programme operation as the 100th television station in the United States and the first non-experimental educationally owned television station in the world, culminating a planned development, begun by President Charles E.A. Fieley in 1945.

The 1951 Federal Communications Commission allocation hearing which were to result in nation-wide reservation of television channels for education and a resolution in American Educational Methods, were about to begin a precursor to a remarkable series of events. In April 1952, as a result of the hearing, the Federal Communications Commission established a new kind of broadcast entity, the non-commercial educational television station, and reserved 242 channels in the broadcast spectrum for use by the educational establishment. In July 1952, Kansas State College applied for permission to construct one of these new stations, though a later applicant was to have a distinction of being first on the air.

CCTV

The growth in educational television and broadcast network was matched by an even more rapid, but least costly development in closed circuit television (CCTV) installations, totaling more than 300. Cable and microwave systems were widely employed for special laboratory applications, observation of university lectures and demonstration and for the formal instruction of regularly enrolled students at all levels. Installations ranged in size from simple room to room on channel cable connections in a single school building to multiple circuit system, complete with studios and video tape recording equipment.

Education Channels

In late 1949, efforts to reserve television channels for education were finally achieving substantial momentum. The United States Office of Education has filed its own petition with the Federal Communications Commission asking that a very high frequency as well as an ultra high frequency (UHF) channels be reserved for education. By 1950, there was a number of supporting national educational groups preparing petitions for education television reservation. Throughout 1950 and 1951 these various educational groups focused their attention on problems of finance and strategy. The National Association of Educational Broadcasters led by George Probst, Director of the University of Chicago "NBC Round Table" and Seymour Director of WNYC and the Municipal Broadcasting System in New York City began a national fund raising campaign. These men, held conversations with C. Scott Fletcher, president of the newly created Fund for the Adult Education, an independent organisation, established by the Ford Foundation. Fletcher and Find keenly aware from the outset of the educational potential of radio and television, immediately saw six areas of desirable supporting activity which could forward and sustain this endeavour.

The American Council on Education enlisted the support and counsel of a comprehensive cross-section of U.S. educational, business, communications and Governmental leadership in the precedent making an "Educational Television Programme Institute" at the University of Pennsylvania. The high point of 1952 occurred when the Federal Communications

Commission issued its six reports and an order which reserved, for the educational establishment, a total of 242 television channels. Shortly thereafter, Kansas State College became the first institute to apply for an educational non-commercial station and in 1953, KVHT at the University of Houston began telecasting programmes.

All these events marked the beginning of a new era in American education. The FCC had finally established a new nation-wide television allocation plan. Two hundred forty two (242) channels were reserved for exclusive non-commercial educational use by schools, colleges, universities and non profit education television operations.

Use of ETV

Television now constitutes an important medium widely used to disseminate information to its viewers. It has the unique feature of combining audio and visual technology and is thus considered to be more effective. It serves multiple purposes of entertainment, information and education. Besides performing motivational function, it helps in providing discovery learning and cognitive development of its viewers. Because of its better accessibility, it can bring learning materials to the masses in more direct, effective and personal ways than other educational media. Although every media has some strengths and weakness, its effectiveness depends more on how it is used. Researches carried out by Bates (1981, 1983, 1987 and 1988), Salomon (1979) and Olson and Bruner (1974) suggest that the television differs from other media in the way that it can represent knowledge, together with its educational and pedagogic implications. This is borne out by various reports.

Use of television as an instructional medium was first reported in 1932 by State University of IOWA in USA on an experimental basis in a world fair. Later on, due to the World War II, the introduction of television slowed down and, as a result, by 1948 there were very few educational institutions involved in using television as an instructional medium in spite of a great interest in television evinced by the educationists. Realizing the power of television for educational purpose, "the Federal Communication Commission in USA reserved 242 frequencies for educational broadcast on no-profit and non-commercial basis in 1952" (Magnuson, 1965).

By the late 1950s, as many as 17 programs used television in their instructional materials. The use of educational television tended to grow slowly but by 1961 about 53 stations were affiliated with the National Educational Television Network (NETT) with the primary goal of coordinating scheduling (Hull, 1962). The number of education television stations grew more rapidly in the 1960s and, by 1972 nearly 233 educational stations existed (Carnegie Commission, 1979),

Ohio University, University of Texas and the University of Maryland were among the earliest universities to create networks' reach for both on-campus and off-campus student populations (Brientenfield, 1968). Some other universities also started considering on how to bring distance learning to select student populations with the help of television.

Hizal (1983) enumerates various functions of television in delivering education through distance mode, like supporting and enhancing teaching; instructing; explaining, clarifying; motivation and encouragement; imposing study speed (determining rate of study); presenting a reference to large masses; changing behaviour and presenting the unreachable facts and events. Television can be an effective tool as distance education delivery system. It can be integrated into the curriculum to provide information either on a single lesson, or a specific unit or even full course. The instructional television can be interactive (allowing the viewers to interact with instructor or other students live) or passive (airing pre-recorded programmes). Lochte (1993) described an experiment using two-way television with two-way audio wherein all students could view and interact with the teacher, and simultaneously, the teacher could view all participating.

Walker (1995) also favoured television for its audio and visual effects and reported that it can be used to demonstrate processes or physical skills; to show movement; to show visual that reflect on the colour depth cues and motion of the object; can be used for those who lack reading skills; help make distance learning more personalized; make teaching-learning attractive and dynamic and is useful for skill development. In addition to the advantages, he highlighted some of the limitations of television of its being primarily a one-way communication medium; broadcast is difficult to integrate with other media; both production and transmission of programmes are costly; production process is very lengthy; and it is restricted with the effective range of the transmitter or satellite.

Satyanarayana & Seshratham (2000) reported on the utilization of the instructional power of television by the U.K. Open University, the pioneer of distance teaching learning system, from the very beginning. The main area of usage of TV in the Open University was in experimental situations; to bring to students primary resource material, i.e. film or video recordings of actual situation; to record special events; experiments, species, places, people, buildings, etc. which are crucial to the content of units, but may be likely to disappear, die or be destroyed in the near future; and to demonstrate the use of tools or equipment, or the efforts of tools or equipmen

The Indian Initiatives

Television first came to India [named as 'Doordarshan'(DD)] on September 15, 1959 as the National Television Network of India. The first telecast started on September 15, 1959 in New Delhi. After a gap of about 13 years, a second television station was established in Bombay in 1972 and by 1975, there were five more television stations at Srinagar (Kashmir), Amritsar (Punjab), Calcutta, Madras and Lucknow. For many years, the transmission was mainly in black and white. Television industry got the necessary boost in the eighties when Doordarshan introduced colour TV during the 1982 Asian Games (http://www.indian television.com/indian broadcast/history/historyoftele.htm). The second phase of growth was witnessed in the early nineties and during the Gulf War, when foreign channels like CNN, Star TV and domestic channels such as Zee TV and Sun TV started broadcast of satellite signal. This changed the scenario and the people got the opportunity to watch regional, national and international programmes. Starting with 41 sets in 1962 and one channel (Audience Research Unit, 1991), at present TV in India covers more than 70 million homes giving a viewing population more than 400 million individuals, through more than 100 channels (http://www.indiantelevison.com). Easy accessibility of relevant technology, variety of programmes and increased hour of transmission are the main reasons for rapid expansion of TV system in India.

3

Major Educational Television Projects

In India, since the inception of TV network, television has been perceived as an efficient force of education and development. With its large audience, it has attracted educators as being an efficient tool for imparting education to primary, secondary and university level students. Some of the major educational television projects are as discussed briefly hereunder:

Secondary School Television Project (1961): This project was designed for the secondary school students of Delhi. With an aim to improve the standard of teaching in view of shortage of laboratories, space, equipment and dearth of qualified teachers in Delhi, this project was started on experimental basis in October 1961 for teaching of Physics, Chemistry, English and Hindi for students of Class XI. The lectures were syllabus based and were telecast during school hours as part and parcel of school activities. According to Paul (1968), 'by and large, the television schools did somewhat better in the test than did the non-television schools'.

The television as demonstrated for the first time in the fair 1959 was for the Indian public. It was first experimental television service in India inaugurated in Delhi to produce and transmit social education programmes under a project aided by UNESCO (Kumar and Chandiram, 1967). With this step forward in the field of telecommunication, India become a member of the group of Asian nations who has started television service of their own. Since some of the teleclubs were located in the schools, the television sets were placed in the schools also. The television viewing facility in such schools thus provided an opportunity for an experiment in school television.

To begin with, a weekly service of specially designed programmes for the benefit of student of class IX was started by AIR from 19th January, 1960 with the collaboration of Education Department of the Delhi Administration.

It was about this time that the representatives of the Ford Foundation were approached by the Government to assist in the development of Educational Television. Towards the end of 1970 India received necessary equipment for strengthening the television service in Delhi. This led to the planning and implementation of an educational TV project for Delhi schools.

During 1965-66, out of Delhi's 320 Higher Secondary schools, 255 were provided with TV sets. According to given table a clear information in regard to the Increase In the TV service.

Delhi Agriculture Television (DATV) Project: Krishi Darshan - 1966

The project named Krishi Darshan was initiated on January 26, (196-) for communicating agricultural information to the farmers on experimental basis for the 80 selected villages of Union Territory of Delhi through 'Community Viewing' of television and further discussions among themselves. The experiment was successful, yielding substantial gain in information regarding agricultural practices (IGNOU, 2000).

Satellite Instructional Television Experiment (SITE - 1975) The project, one of the largest techno-social experiments In human communication, was commissioned on August 1, 1975, for a period of one year for the villagers and the Primary School going children of selected 2330 villages in six states of

India, namely Rajasthan, Karnataka, Orissa, Bihar, Andhra Pradesh and Madhya Pradesh. The main objectives of this experiment were to study the process of existing rural communications, the role of television as new medium of education and the process of change brought about by community television in the rural structure, with following two types of telecast:

1. Developmental education programmes In the area of agriculture and allied subjects, health, family planning and social education, which were telecast in the evening for community viewing.
2. The school programmes of 22½ minutes' duration each in Hindi, Kannada, Oriya and Telugu were telecast on each school day for rural primary school children of 5-12 years age-group to make the children realize the importance of science in their day-to-day life.

SITE experiment showed that the new technology made it possible to reach number of people in the remotest areas. The role of television was appreciated and it was accepted in rural primary schools as an educational force (IGNOU, 2000).

Post-SITE Project (1977)

The target group for this post-SITE project was the villagers of Rajasthan. This was a SITE continuity project and was initiated in March 1977 when a terrestrial transmitter was commissioned at Jaipur. The main objectives of SITE continuity project were to:

1. Familiarize the rural masses with the improved and scientific know-how about farming, the use of fertilizers and the maintenance of health and hygiene;
2. Bring about national and emotional integration; and
3. Make rural children aware of the importance of education and healthy environment.

Indian National Satellite Project (INSAT - 1982)

The prime objective of the INSAT project was aimed at making the rural masses aware of the latest developments in the areas of agricultural productivity, health and hygiene. It was initially targeted at villagers and their school going children of selected villages in Orissa, Andhra Pradesh, Bihar, Gujarat, Maharashtra and Uttar Pradesh. As a part of INSAT of Education project, ETV broadcasts were inaugurated and continued through terrestrial transmission from 15 August 1982 in Orissa and Andhra Pradesh. Later, other states, namely Bihar, Gujarat, Maharashtra and Uttar Pradesh were covered under INSAT service, using INSAT-IB in June 1983. In each state, a cluster of 3-4 districts were selected on the basis of backwardness of the area, availability of suitable developmental infrastructure and utilization of existing production facilities.

Besides developmental programmes for community viewing, educational programmes (ETV) for two different age groups of school children (5-8) and (9-11) years are telecast daily. A capsule of 45 minutes duration consisting of two separate programmes - one for the lower age group and the other for the upper age group - are telecast regularly. Each programme runs for a duration of 20 minutes with five minutes change over time from one age group to the other. As of today, these ETV programmes are offered in five languages - Oriya, Telugu, Marathi, Gujarati and Hindi - for a large population of primary school children. Programmes telecast in Hindi are being received in all Hindi-speaking states in the northern belt (IGNOU, 2000).

UGC-Higher Education Television Project (HETV - 1984)

University students are the beneficiaries of this project. The University Grants Commission in collaboration with INSAT started an educational television project, popularly known as 'Country-wide Classroom' on August 15, 1984, with the aim to update, upgrade and enrich the quality of education while extending their reach. Under this programme, a one-hour programme in English on a variety of subjects is presented with the objective of general enrichment of undergraduates, educated public and the teachers as well. An inter-university Consortium for Education Communication (CEC) along with a chain of about 20 Audio-Visual Research Centres and Mass Communication Research Centres were set up by the UGC at different universities in the country, to ascertain high quality of programming for this project. Besides producing programmes at these centres, some programmes are imported from other countries, and are edited to suit the requirements of the Indian students. This project is very popular among students, teachers and other learners.

IGNOU-Doordarshan Telecast (1991)

The IGNOU-Doordarshan telecast programmes, designed mainly for distance learners, started in May 1991. Initially, they were telecast on every Monday, Wednesday and Friday from 6.30 to 7.00 a.m. through the national network of Doordarshan with the aim of providing tele-counseling to students of open universities in remote areas. Hailing the encouraging response from viewers, the frequency of this project has been increased to five days a week. This programme is now very popular.

Gyan-Darshan Educational Channel (2000)

Ministry of Human Resource Development, Information & Broadcasting, the Prasar Bharti and IGNOU launched Gyan Darshan (GD) jointly on 26th January, 2000 as an exclusive Educational TV Channel of India. IGNOU was given the responsibility to be the nodal agency for u plinking/ transmission. It started out as a two-hour daily test transmission channel for students of open and conventional universities. This duration was increased, in February, to nine hours a day. The time slot in transmission was further increased due to good response upto 16-hours by 1st June and by 1st November, it turned out to be 19-hours channel. Within one year of its launching on 26th January, 2001, it has become a non-stop daily 24 hours transmission channel for educational programmes. "The programming constitutes 23 hours of indigenous programmes, sourced from partner institutions and one our of foreign programmes. Transmission of 12 hours each for curriculum based and enrichment programmes is being made. The programmes of IGNOU, CIET-NCERT including NOS are telecast for four hours each, IIT programmes for three hours, CEC-UGC programmes for two and a half hours and one hour each for TITI and Adult Education" (IGNOU Profile - 2002). The signal for Gyan Darshan transmission are up linked from the Earth Station (augmented as one plus one system set up at IGNOU Hqs., New Delhi and down linked all over the country through INSAT 3C on C Band Transponder. Although Gyan Darshan has made its presence felt in all Open Universities and most of the prominent conventional universities/schools, it still has the potential to reach the doorsteps of le.arners through cable TV network. At present, Gyan Darshan through the cable transmission covers above 90 percent in Kerala, most parts of Tamil Nadu, a few pockets in the North East, Nasik, Ahmedabad and Pune. Asia Net has been providing it free of cost in Kerala. Efforts are being made to make Gyan Darshan available through terrestrial transmission.

Role of Television for Globalization of Education

With the aid of latest information technology, educational jurisdiction of the institutions has expanded for beyond their geographical proximity. The universities have started thinking internationally as regards their curriculum and course contents. Global universities are emerging bringing together students and faculty from many countries through satellite television.

So educational television is a means by which we can get education through foreign experts at home and with the help of its other languages can be learnt easily.

EDUSAT

EDUSAT is the first Indian satellite built exclusively for serving the educational sector. It is mainly intended to meet the demand for an interactive satellite based distance education system for the country. It is strongly reflects India's commitment to use space technology for national development, especially for the development of the population in remote and rural locations.

EDUSAT is the first exclusive satellite for serving the educational sector. It is specially configured for audio-visual medium, employing digital interactive classroom and multimedia multicentric system. The satellite will have multiple regional beams covering different parts of India -

five Ku-band transponders with spot beams covering northern, north-eastern, southern and western regions of the country, a Ku-band transponder with its footprint covering the Indian mainland region and six C-band transponders with their footprints covering the entire country.

EDUSAT is primarily meant for providing connectivity to school, college and higher levels of education and also to support non-formal education including developmental communication. The scope of the EDUSAT programme is planned to be realized in three parts.

In the first phase of pilot projects, a Ku-band transponder on board INSAT-3B, which is already in orbit, is being used. In this phase, Visveswaraiah Technological University (VTY) in Karnataka, Y B Chavan State Open University in Maharashtra and the Rajiv Gandhi Technical University in Madhya Pradesh are covered. In the second phase, EDUSAT spacecraft, once commissioned in orbit, will be used in a semi-operational mode with at least one uplink in each of the five spot beams. About 100-200 classrooms will be connected in each beam. Coverage will be extended to two more states and one national institution. In the third phase, EDUSAT network is expected to become fully operational. ISRO will provide technical and managerial support in the replication of EDUSAT ground systems to manufacturers and service providers. End users are expected to provide funds for this. In this phase, ground infrastructure to meet the country's educational needs will be built and during this period, EDUSAT will be able to support about 25 to 30 up links and about 5000 remote terminals per uplink.

While ISRO will provide the space segment for EDUSAT System and demonstrate the efficacy of the satellite system for interactive distance education, content generation is the responsibility of the user agencies. The quantity and quality of the content would ultimately decide the success of EDUSAT System. This involves an enormous effort by the user agencies. To help in this, ISRO, in cooperation with the user agencies, has already organised five conferences at the regional level, one at the national level and one conference of vice-chancellors of Indian universities to create awareness about the EDUSAT and its capabilities. The latest conference at Bangalore was jointly organised by ISRO and the Association of Indian Universities in July, 2004. The indigenous realization and launch of EDUSAT will provide a substantial boost to countrywide distance education in India.

5

Television and wide Range of Instruction Strategies

With the help of ETV we can teach to the children with the help of different types of strategies. Instruction has not remained confined to classroom lectures only. New instructional strategies like role playing, simulation, etc. for socio-emotional skills, values and effects, panel discussion, interview, live scene/events to make knowledge better intelligible and receivable are selling wide spread application through television.

With the help of ETV new instructional principles with their illustrations of field application are generated.

Use of the best Available Teacher

Educational television makes educational opportunities equal throughout the country. The students in the rural and deprived areas of the country where educational resources are not available get the quality of education as their counterparts in the urban centres. The best teacher is equally available for every student. This television bridges the gap between the poor and the rich, the privileged and the unprivileged, the rural and the urban.

- **Cost Effective:** If television is utilized on a large scale, it proves cost effective. It can provide education throughout the country at a minimum cost without lowering the quality of instruction.

- **Logistically Simple:** In operating an effective distance education system, educational television is logistically very simple, the problem of planning, implementing and operating distance learning can be overcome to some extent by teaching through television.
- **Combination of Audio and Video Components:** Television has the advantage of the audio and video. That is why it has a greater appeal the radio and the print media.
- **Simulation:** Through educational television, we can control the stimulation (the audio and the visual) to get desired response (learning).

Need of the Study

The need of ETV programmes may be essential to tide over the shortcomings of the conventional method. A good medium is an important factor in education. If education is to win in the race, all available resources of the world will need to be mobilized to accept the challenges of science and technology and thus, create a better world. Good education is extremely important for the survival and improvement of democracy in the world. Thus, effective educational programmes through television may help in this regards. But what really makes ETV effective still remains an open question.

In the context of EFA or universal primary education, the effectiveness of ETV programme is primarily related to the students achievement in Mathematics and General Science, besides language proficiency. In this era, however, when the technology is leaping to its great height, the role of mathematics and science takes the central stage. In order to boost scientific temper among students at this stage of their development and to encourage them to pursue the path of reflective work their achievement in mathematics and science is considered to be of vital importance. Hence, this study to analyze and evaluate the impact of electronic media, particularly, ETV on successfully achieving the goal of universal primary education.

In the face of educational television and software technology becoming important day by day, television sets are being increasingly installed in schools all over the country, with educational television centres telecasting programmes on various subjects and topics crucial to the course content as well as to the preparation for life, in general. The focus of the study is thus concerned with the impact of educational telecast on primary school students especially in relation to their achievement in mathematics and science. It is aimed at throwing light on the popularity and effectiveness of the television lesson on personality development of the primary school children m Delhi, especially in terms of their achievement and attitude vis-a-vis ETV programmes.

Research Gap

So far limited efforts have been made in India to highlights these issues especially in the context of ETV In primary education in rural and urban areas. There have been a few studies conducted on SIET project by Agarwal (1978), Mohanty and Giri (1977), Mody (1978), Rahman (1977), Shukla and Kumar (1977) and Mohanty & Mohanty (1984) with focus on coverage of ETV programmes at target group level as well as impact of different types of educational programmes in viewers behaviour. On school level ETV there have been studies on utilisation of programmes like Piagnkar (1978), CIET (1984), Goel (1984), Singh and Umare (1986) with concentration of area coverage of schools, time-table attendance of learners, regularity in use, etc. There are a number of studies which explore opinion of viewer students as well as teachers on the quality of ETV programmes at school stage such as Shah (1972), EIET (1984b), Goel (1984), Jaiswal (1988), Mohanty & Mohanty, Suriakant and Meenakshi (1989), Sainathambi (1990). Moreover, experiments have been conducted on effectiveness of one way communication mode of ETV on different sample groups of learners, with achievement as major criteria of achievement. They have not explored that affect appropriate strategies for integration of

ETV programmes in school activities as well as effectiveness of ETV. This study concentrates on exploring such factors as well as studying comparative effectiveness of ETV and traditional mode.

Rationale of the Present Study

In recent years, television is being utilized increasingly by developed as well as developing countries to meet the growing demand for education and to improve and enrich instruction. In India, television entered into the field of education in 1959, but it started systematic telecasting of educational programmes at school level after the successful launching of INSAT -1B in 1983.

As highlighted above, ETV has occupied a major place in modern educational technology. Several issues can be raised in the context of ETV at school stage, that - that are the factors that come on the way of use of ETV at primary school stage? It is high time to see that factors affecting effectiveness, efficiency and utilization of ETV in terms of achievement goals in general and instructional objective in specific. It is essential for school teachers to consider:

1. Why they should use television for certain areas of curriculum;
2. "Whether the series and programmes intended for use fit in with the curriculum policies of the school; and
3. How the viewing session will be incorporated with day to day teaching learning activities of schools.

Since primary education system is decentralized in the country questions are to be answered through empirical studies conducted in the country. Whether the user learners benefit from ETV in the context of appreciation of new technology in general and development of positive attitude towards ETV in specific will indicate another dimension of effectiveness of ETV.

The success of ETV will depend upon internal quality of programmes, i.e. language content relevance, visuals, audio, synchronization of audio-video, etc. Scrutiny of these aspects of ETV programme-wise by the participants as well as teacher will be useful in developing totalistic picture about effectiveness of ETV.

As known in general ETV is a modern technology. This is also hypothesized that those who have better acquaintance with new technologies like Radio, TV and Computer may find it flexible to participate in the process of learning through ETV which may lead to better learning outcomes than their non or less technology acquaintance counterparts.

This study has been undertaken with a view to providing valuable suggestion for between planning and organisation of the educational system in general and effective utilisation of educational television programmes in particular. The findings of the study will help in effective planning, production, utilisation and evaluation of educational television programmes.

- In Delhi.
- Both male and female students and teacher were included.
- The utilisation of the ETV programmes was studied only in primary schools of Delhi.
- The study was restricted to teaching of Mathematics, Environmental Education (EVS).

Literature Related to Educational Television

Introduction

The review of literature has a creative and analytical function. According to Good, Barr and Scates, the review is essential for developing valid in sights in the area of the study and also for projecting tentative solution to the problem while Borg is of the opinion that related literature provides the infrastructure from which the study grows and a perspective against which it should be assessed. Bruce Tuchman says that the review of related literature is an essential device for developing an adequate research spectrum. Thus, keeping in view the importance of review of related literature, this chapter is devoted to the same.

Since the present study alms at utilization and effectiveness of ETV programmes at the primary level, the investigator extensively probed into vast expanse of research conducted on ETV programmes at different levels in India and abroad. This has yielded such enormous volume of data that it is difficult to decide upon the studies to be reviewed. For the purpose of objectivity and simplicity, the related research was categorized into two groups - one group comprising studies related to provision and utilization of ETV and the other group comprising studies related to effectiveness of ETV programmes.

The aim of entire exercise of reviewing literature was to provide direction and evolve a rationale for formulation of hypotheses for the present study.

Studies on Provision and Utilization of ETV Facilities

Deiong, E.L. (1975) conducted a study on "Future utilization of TV in Texas Public School". To identify expected trends in television utilization in "Texas Public School". Data were collected on your aspects of television utilization. The future of TV in the classroom and the future use of TV in non-classroom situation. The types of television distribution systems to be used and the area of coverage of these distribution systems. Responses of these distribution systems responses of the Texas group and the National group registered a 96% agreement in predicting the years in which developing trends will achieve and revealed that trends in classroom utilization of television will include placing a television receiver or receptacle in each classroom, integrated television into the learning climate, bringing the community into the classroom, projecting visual materials and individualizing instruction.

Saulat Rahman (1977) reported the most significant finding of the study that was conducted by the University of Education, Government of India in collaboration with the Educational Technology Cell, Orissa and Doordarshan Kendrea, Cuttack to study the liking of ETV programmes among the teaches and children. It was a summative study taking a large sample representative of all three clusters of the state of Orissa as revealed that: there was high liking of the programmes among children and teaches. There was a variation among children and teachers. A good script based on the careful structuring of ideas is essential for good television programmes.

Akutsu and Others (1978) conducted a study on the factors related to the use of STV at the elementary level in Japan. The revealed that there are some factors which until now have not been given a great deal of consideration in regards to the utilisation of school television programmes. It included the STV programmes, strategies use and environmental factors. Major findings are: in those schools which did not use TV school programme regularly, it was the female teachers who used it more. Teachers who used a great deal of TV did not feel compulsion to improve their instruction. The role of the principal was important to the use of STV. In school strategies were more effective in getting teachers to use school TV than research meeting to classroom observation. Ghiossi (1978) of the Florida State University conducted a study to survey the opinions of social studies teachers in Shiraz (Iran) regarding the potential use of television in their instructional activities. The result of the experiment showed positive effect of the teachers' academic degree on their attitude towards the instructional television. That is, the teachers with higher level of academic degree stand to use more of instructional television than the teachers with associated degrees who was later supervisor over teachers with high school diploma.

Bostic (1984) conducted a study of the use of ITV in Mississippi Public School of U.S.A. The purpose of this study was to determine the extent of use of ITV by public school teachers in Mississippi. The sample was selected from teachers who taught K.G. through grade II. It revealed that college credit hours in ITV availability of informative materials about ITV such as teachers guides, schedules, etc. attending meeting, workshop or conference on ITV were positively related to use of ITV.

Taglides (1984) of Southern Illinois University at Carbondale conducted a study n the attitude of Greek parents and teachers towards sex-education via educational television. The purpose of the study was to measure and compare parents and teachers attitude towards sex education for primary school children, towards ETV as a medium of instruction and towards the audio and video message of sex education programme utilized by Greek ETV revealed that parents and teachers had a favourable attitude both toward sex education for primary school children and towards ETV as medium of instruction. The difference in the means of their attitude was not statistically significant. Parents and teachers demonstrated a favourable attitude towards the audio and video messages of the sex education programme. The review of the study indicated a positive effect of teachers' education programmes on teachers' professional growth, development of their favourable attitudes.

Singh and Singh (1984) conducted a study "to assess the needs of the primary school children of Orissa for ETV support". After taking the sample: 75% of the teachers by and large, favoured the use of such ETV programmes as are only or mostly syllabus based for the children of I to V, while many (20%) also favoured the use of ETV for exposing children to the programmes of general nature. The syllabus based TV programmes would help the children learn topics included in the syllabus more effectively. Since the rural children were generally not able to understand telecast based on unfamiliar topics or outside their experience it would be easy to the children to understand familiar subjects and to motivate them to learn more. So giving their preference to syllabus based programmes, a number of teacher felt that EVS students of classes I and II and general science for classes III, IV and V might be given to priority for classes to III. It would be satisfying if the syllabus based programmes and general programmes are telecast in the ratio of 3: 1.

Utilization of the ETV programmes in Maharashtra State was studied by Sudame and Goel (1985). Stratified sampling was selected. A questionnaire was developed by the researchers for the Headmasters and mailed to the schools. According to the response of questionnaires the findings of the study remarks TV sets are out of order with no special provision for their repairs. The support materials such as STY programme schedule, teachers' notes, etc. were not received by the schools in time. Pre and post-telecast activities were not carried out by the school teachers. Most of the school teachers were not trained in utilizing the STY programmes for classroom instruction. Most of the teachers and students have positive creation regarding the STY programmes.

Choat, Criffin and Narbart (1986) conducted a study, whether the ETV programmes were used by the teachers effectively in England and Wales into the way of ETV was used by 259 teachers and children upto the age of seven years indicated that only a few teachers were using the medium effectively as the class viewing and mass viewing of programmes remained the normal methods, even when a video recorder was used for time table convenience. The finding indicated the need for an initial training of teaches and for a vastly increased in-service programme for serving teachers and provision of adequate resources.

Sudalnik James E. (1986) conducted a study on the development and utilization of cable television in eight southern California campuses of the California State University. The purpose of the study was to document the criterion and current utilisation of table television as a resource on eight southern California Campuses of the California State University system.

Because 80% institutes of higher education was beginning to utilize cable television as a means of disseminating various types of information and instruction the review of the literature was used to trace the historical development of educational ratio and television broadcasting as well as the development of cable television industry. Current and potential uses of the cable as an educational resource were described. So a combination of the historical survey and case study methodology was used. The findings indicated all eight institution utilize cable television in varying degrees for a variety of purposes including information dissemination, promotion, instruction and classification support material. It was also found that cable television enhances certain curricular programmes.

Chu and Schramm (1987) conducted a study on the attitudes of teachers and pupils. The research evidence makes attitudes towards instructional television seem rather more favourable than one would expect from the experience reports that circulate. So teachers and pupils are more favourable towards the use of ITV than in secondary school level and college. Administrators are more favourable towards ITV than are teachers. At the college level, students tend to prefer small discussion classes to teaching class, television class to large lecture classes.

Chaudhary, S. Sohanvir (1990) conducted a study of teachers attitude towards STY and its relationship with mass media behaviour and job satisfaction. To study the attitude of teachers towards school television as an educational sub-system. To study the relationship between the teachers attitude and his job satisfaction. To study the influence of the personal and academic characteristics of teachers in relation to their attitude towards school television. The sample comprised primary school teachers of 104 villages having television. The tools were attitude scale and interview schedule. "t" test and ANOVA and Chi Square were used. The custodian teachers, on the whole, had a fairly favourable attitude towards STY. Teachers supported the effect of visuals on students. They perceived STY as an effective learning medium. The teachers who taught the higher classes (IV and V) have more favourable attitude towards STV.

Anuradha, K. (1991) conducted a study on children's television viewing behaviour and its effect on personal and educational development. To develop tools to measure television viewing behaviour (TVB) and attitude towards television viewing (ATTV). To compare parents and children's viewpoints with regard to TV viewing and to explore the potential influence of TV viewing on the educational development. The sample of the study comprised 180 children who had TV in their homes. Schedules for parents and children and Intellectual Achievement scale were used to collect data. It was found that 90% of the students were light viewers.

There were no heavy viewers. The students spent more time on seeing sports and advertisement. A majority of children disagreed that TV affected their school work and they became disinterested in serial work. They felt that TV viewing helped a lot in school work, and they gained more knowledge and consequently got good marks.

Arularam (1991) conducted a study to verify how far the objectives of the UGC country-wise ETV have been put in practical. To verify the extent to which the UGC country-wide ETV enriched knowledge utilized the potentiality of the TV medium and catered to the needs of target population. The sample comprised rural undergraduate students who were drawn using cluster sampling method. The researcher used observation schedule as a tool to collect the relevant data. Only a quarter of the telecast time was allotted to foreign programmes. The humanitarian programmes provided in India offered the least knowledge enrichment.

Ghosh, Sunanda (1992) conducted a study to provide details regarding educational reporting on TV in Tamil Nadu state. Educational programmes shown on TV have been surveyed and analysed. As regards quality the UGC programmes were technically sophisticated, specially when the foreign made programmes were shown. Twenty-one hours were devoted to Educational programmes, though many of them were not telecast in the "prime viewers time".

Studies Related to Impact of ETV Programmes

Praziev and Evan (1960) conducted a study to measure the effectiveness of Educational TV programmes in elementary science for the teachers and children of third and fourth grade in Ohio. After viewing the television programmes the teachers reported that they themselves had significantly greater confidence in teaching elementary science and the pupils also should greater interest in it. But a test of achievement showed no significant increase in the children's score.

Ogawa (1960) conducted a study on educational television programme. To compare the pre-test and post-test; to know difference in the students knowledge. 140 Japanese fifth grade children watch an educational TV programme about the Tokyo- Yokohama institutional area. Comparison of pre-test and post-test showed substantial increase in the student's knowledge.

Welbur Schramn (1975) conducted a follow-up study on the achievement data of students in primary, secondary and post secondary education in different subject matters and showed that while there were no significant difference among subject matters taught, younger children learned more from television than older ones. He studies the attitudes of students and teachers towards television. Both faculty and students showed more favourable attitude towards teaching and learning via television.

Butler, Robert, Ryon (1980) conducted a study on the comparative analysis of three instructional television presentation formats. The subjects of the study were 287 fourth grade students grouped into four treatment categories each consisting of three intact classes. The first three groups specified as experimental classes, received television instruction, which presented the same content to each by different method. The three styles utilized were a lecture demonstration method format (Group I), a narrated version (Group II) and a still picture presentation (Group III). The control group received no instruction via television. Each of the three group received the pre-test, the post-test and different treatment. The control group received only the tests. Cognitive learning from televised instruction is more effective produced when certain types of presentation formats are embodied. In Educational Television programmes, greater learning from instruction television occurs when viewers' attention is highlighted. Teachers were enthusiastic towards ITV produce a positive acceptance of televised instruction in their students.

Clemeus (1982) conducted a study on the relationship between television viewing, selected students characteristics and academic achievement. The major intent of the study was to determine which students may be most vulnerable to television's effects. Data as the part of 1981 Pennsylvania Educational Quality Assessment for students in grade five, eight and eleven were analysed to determine the relationship between the amount of television and academic achievement. A consistent pattern of negative correlation between the amount of television viewing and academic achieve men t existed for all groups examined in this study, although television viewing accounted for only a small percentage of the variable in achievement, a significant relationship existed between the amount of television viewing and academic achievement for sub-groups based on sex, race, type of commerce and socio-economic status. A substantial drop in the mean scores achievement occurred when the students watched five or more hours television daily.

Seth (1983) conducted a study on the impact of ETV programmes with and without teachers introduction on primary schools in Delhi. To study the difference among three groups. First the children those without ETV. Second the comparison between. the children who watch ETV with the support of teacher's introduction and without support of teacher's introduction. The children exposed to TV gave better language development, higher organisation of information compared with the group that did not watch ETV. The group that received the programmes with support from teachers, in the form of introduction of the programme and follow up work after the telecast achieved still higher on all the three variables mentioned above.

Singh and Singh (1983) conducted a study on the impact of the ETV programmes on the children of class IV and V in Sambalpur District (Orissa). The study revealed that ITV was helpful in imparting useful information to the children of class VI and V of the rural schools. The children of TV schools did better on the achievement test in social studies and science compared to the children of the non-TV schools. Whether the TV had a similar potential in bringing about language development and attitudinal change on the part of the children could not be ascertained. So using a powerful mass medium like TV in primary education need to bring about language development among the children by exposing them to the standard languages.

Torres (1984) of the Pennsylvania State University conducted a study on the effect of the TV programmes on the prospective teachers. The main purpose was to determine whether the pre-service teachers training was transmitting adequate knowledge of bilingual education; developing attitudes towards pre-service training and providing an adequate perception of the goals of bilingual education in the student-teachers, revealed, as result of an experimental and control group treatments with pre and post-test design on 400 student-teachers of the state by administering the test of knowledge of bilingual education and attitudes questionnaire towards pre-service training. Thus the level of knowledge acquired by the participants was significantly higher than non-participants. The attitude towards pre-service training was more favourable in the experimental group and no significance difference was found with regard to goal perception of bilingual education.

Mohanty, P.C. (1988) conducted a study to assess the impact of Educational TV programmes in three districts of Orissa. The main objectives were: to study the impact of ETV programmes on the scholastic achievement of primary school children and to study the operational credibility of the medium of TV, particularly that of ETV programmes. A sample of 30 control schools from all the three cluster districts was drawn randomly and 300 subjects were further drawn at random for treatment conditions. The total number of teachers interviewed from TV non-TV schools was 300. The tools were three achievement tests which were developed to assess the impact of ETV programmes. Questionnaires, check-list and an interview schedule were developed to get the feedback from teachers and Headmasters. The collected data were treated by using mean, S.D., CR and ANOVA. The experimental group had superior mean achievement scores as compared to the control group which indicated the expected impact of educational television on the scholastic achievement of primary school children in respect of gaining knowledge in science, social studies and language.

Behera, S.C. (1990) conducted a study to investigate the impact of educational television programmes on the competency of teachers belonging to elementary schools. To study the impact of ETV on the competency of teaches of elementary schools in terms of knowledge, understanding and application in content areas. Classroom interaction between teacher and students. Attitudes of teachers towards ETV programmes. To see the problems of the teachers with respect to the utilisation of the ETV programmes. Twenty five TV schools as experimental schools with 50 teachers and 25 non-TV schools as control schools with fifty teachers were taken as sample schools. In addition 25 of the inspecting officers concerned were also selected to provide data about the problems of TV utilization. Achievement test, Flanders' Interaction Opinionnaire, Feedback Schedule were used. There was a great difference between the TV and non-TV teachers on their knowledge, understanding and application in the covered content areas. The attitude of the teachers towards ETV revealed that a highly sufficient chunk of teachers considered ETV as not only an effective medium but also conducive to teaching and development of teachers knowledge and general awareness.

Phutela, R.L. (1991) conducted a study to assess the effects of comics and comic television serials on children. To survey various types of available comic books and comic television serials. To find out the extent of reading viewing on the part of children. To study their likes and dislikes regarding comic books/serials. Data were collected from cross-section of 198 children. 19 teachers and 17 parents, taking 25 children each from classes III and VI from six schools. Tools comprised a questionnaire, checklist and rating scale. Class III students liked stories on magic the most, followed by those of horror, animals, fools and silly dolls, etc. Class VI or older children, the liking was in the order: stories on magic, fools and silly. Most teachers felt that comics were useful in many ways, whereas 10% considered these passive materials as fostering undesirable values. Among the six cartoon television serials, the percentages of preferences for class III and VI, respectively were Mickey Mouse.

Sahoo, P.K., Mallick (1993) conducted a study on attitude of rural primary school children towards ETV. To study the level of attitude of primary school children towards ETV; to study the effect of level, technology acquaintance and sex background of students on attitudes of ETV. The sample comprised of 90 students, 45 each from classes III and V. Self constructed attitude scale were used to collect the data. Mean, S.D. and 't' test were calculated for analyzing the data. There was no significant difference between the mean attitude scores of upper primary and lower primary stage. Technology acquaintance had significant effect on the attitude of students towards ETV. Sex background of the students had a significant effect on attitude towards ETV.

Holly R. Rudlph and Robert Ascay (1998) conducted a study on "Interactive Television: A Reassessment of student performance and attitudes in an upper division accountancy course. To study the impact of ITV on collegiate hearing and found that ITV medium of instruction had an initial negative impact on students performance, but as students gained experience the negative effect diminished and became insignificant. The changes and advancement in ITV instruction since then promoted this re-examination.

Jaiswal, K. (1992) conducted a study of higher education, science education television programmes in terms of their contents, presentation, students' reactions and effectiveness. To analyse the higher education science educational television programmes in terms of their contents and presentation. To find out the effectiveness of the higher education science ETV programmes in terms of students' achievement and find out students' reactions to higher education science ETV programmes. The B.Ed. and Computer Diploma students were taken. The sample students were administered achievement tests on the basis of such analysis. Chi Square and 't' tests were employed to treat the data. Most of the programme focused on knowledge and on understanding objectives. The majority of programmes had followed a logical sequence in presentation lecture with demonstration and illustration was quite effective.

Recent Indian Studies on Effectiveness of ETV

Agarwal, R. (1995) in the doctoral study titled "A comparative study of conceptual understanding by programmed instruction and computer assisted instruction" conducted on a sample of 160 students of Class IX (boys and girls both) from ASC Central School, Bareilly revealed that:

1. Both the methods - PI and CAI were quite effective for teaching biological concepts to Class IX students regardless of their sex, intelligence or SES level.
2. Neither the level of conceptual understanding nor the time taken for learning by PI group students was influenced by their sex, intelligence or SES level.
3. CAI method was not equally beneficial to all the students. It was better for boys, students of higher intelligence and students belonging to high socio-economic status group.
4. For concept teaching, CAI method was more effective than PI method only in case of boys, students of average and high intelligence and those belonging to upper strata of society. Otherwise, PI method was as good as CAI method even better than CAI method for less intelligent students.
5. Sex did not determine the learning speed of students when concepts were taught through CAI method.
6. Intelligence and SES were effective determinants for the time effectiveness of CAI method. It was better for higher intelligence and higher SES groups.

7. CAI method was less time consuming for students than the PI method.
8. Students showed favourable attitude towards both the methods but they, particularly the girls, were more inclined towards CAI method than to PI method.

Chandra, Arvinda and Pandya, Rameshari (1996) in "How effective are video films for imparting legal education?" attempted to study the effectiveness of video films for imparting legal education in order to develop an effective introductory course and video instructional package on 'Women and Law' and to study the effectiveness of video package to teach the subject to the First Year Home Science students in terms of performance of students on knowledge test. It revealed that:

1. Majority of the students were from general stream having urban background with social science inclination and majority did not possess legal and social work background.
2. Majority of the respondents were modern and extraverts although their mothers were housewives.
3. Nearly equal percentage of respondents were having high as well as low exposure to TV and video.
4. Marjory of the students were from high socio-economic status and nearly 60 percent had high English competence, but low academic achievement.
5. All the seven video films were effective as there was considerable increase in the mean scores of the students' achievement on post-test for all the seven video films.
6. Overall, the film 'Trauma of Rapel' was found to be most effective and film on 'Introduction to Law' was least effective.
7. The science stream respondents gained significantly higher than the general stream respondents on all the seven video films.

8. There was a significant difference in gain in knowledge of students from English medium school as they learnt more in comparison to the students from vernacular schools.
9. Respondents who had science inclination learnt significantly higher than the respondents having social science inclination.
10. The respondents from city learnt significantly higher from the film 'Are you eve-teased?' For rest of the films, variable 'place of residence' did not play any role.
11. The film 'Marriage made easy with Law was found to be the most effective by the respondents who mothers were housewives.
12. The effect of variable, English competence was found to be significant for all the seven video films.
13. The respondents from high socio-economic status gained significantly higher from the video films in comparison to students from middle and low socio-economic groups.
14. There was no significant difference in learning in relation to social work background, TV and video exposure, modernity, academic achievement and personality.

In a doctoral level experimental study on "Effectiveness of instructor controlled interactive video as compared to conventional non-interactive video and lecture method in modifying the cognitive behaviour among farmers in agriculture" conducted on a sample of 150 farmers (three groups each of 50 farmers) from three villages of the Kanyakumari District of Tamil Nadu, Enigo, M. Charles (1977) revealed that:

1. There was a significant difference between the means of pre-and post-test scores of the Control-Experimental Groups at all levels of cognition in the selected content areas of agriculture, in favour of the post-test scores.

2. ICIV was more effective than LM in modifying the cognitive behaviour among farmers at all levels except at understanding level. ICIV was also more effective as compared to CNIV in modifying the cognitive behaviour. Further, LM was found to be more effective than CNIV in modifying the cognitive behaviour.
3. Irrespective of the difficulty levels of content areas, ICIV was found to be more effective as compared to LM and CNIV in modifying the cognition.
4. Irrespective of the programme formats, ICIV was found to be more effective as compared to CNIV in modifying the cognitive behaviour.
5. ICIV was found to be more effective in its effectiveness in enhancing retention at all levels of cognition except at understanding level as compared to LM and ICIV was relatively more effective than CNIV.
6. Straight Talk enhanced better retention as compared to documentary and any other programme format.

Joshi, Anuradha and Mahapatra, B.C. (1995) in an empirical study on "Effectiveness of computer software in terms of higher mental ability of school children in science" conducted on a sample of 67 students studying in Class IX from Indore Public School and Rising Star Higher Secondary School, Indore revealed that the adjusted mean higher mental ability scores in science of the students taught through developed software package was significantly better from those taught through traditional method when intelligence was taken as covariate.

In a doctoral level experimental study of effect of media on student learning, Parhar, M. (1994) examined the impact of school television on student learning in reference to objectives like:

1. to carry out a survey of media (STV and RCCP) facilities and their utilization in schools;

2. to construct a set of objective, valid and reliable achievement tests in English, mathematics, science for Class VII;
3. to study the impact of media on student learning in English, mathematics and science for Class VII;
4. to study the effect of media on learning vis-a- vis socio-economic background of students; and
5. to suggest measures for improving media impact.

The experiment was conducted on a sample of 341 students of Class VII, with 158 in the control group (non-user schools) and 183 in the experimental group (user-school), from four user schools and four non-user schools. The sample of schools was selected randomly. Tools used included a self-made questionnaire, Achievement tests in science, mathematics and English and self-made observation schedule and the socio-economic status blank of Kuppuswamy. It revealed that:

1. out of the 20 schools chosen, only four were found to be using school television programmes fully, while radio-cum-cassette players were not being used by these schools. No teacher was found to be trained in the usage of school television programme;
2. the mean scores in mathematics as well as science in four experimental schools differed from the control group but not significantly; and
3. The mean difference In English achievement between the user group or non-user group was not significant.

In a doctoral level experimental study in "Effectiveness of computer assisted instruction in teaching physics at higher secondary stage" conducted on a sample of 120 class XII students, Rangaraj, K.R. (1977) revealed that:

1. there were significant differences between the means of pre- and post-test in physics among one control and two experimental groups at all the levels of cognition in favour of the post-test;

2. there was significant difference between the means of CAI-SS and PAI as individualized instruction and conventional lecture method by the post-test. The mean of the CAl-SS was found to be greater than the CAl as individualized instruction and conventional lecture method;
3. there was significant difference between the means of the scores of the pupils at all levels of cognition as measured by the retention test between lecture method and CAI as individualized instruction and CAI as SS, and also between CAI as individualized instruction and CAl as SS;
4. there was no significant difference between the means of the high and low range scores classified, based on different psychological variables with regard to their academic achievement in physics for the groups of CAI as individualized instruction and CAI as SS; and
5. there was no significant difference between the means of the groups of CAI as individualized instruction and CAI as support system on the scores of the pupils on psychological variables as measured by the post-test.

Singh, Ummed (1995) in his experimental study on "Video-instructional package to develop environmental awareness in secondary schools" conducted on a sample of 180 Hindi medium students studying in Classes VII and VIII selected randomly from schools of Surat, Churu and Bareilly found that:

1. The study resulted in the development of a video-instructional package on "Environmental Crisis" for creating environmental awareness among school-going children of Hindi medium schools;
2. The developed video-instructional package was found significantly effective for the students of Classes VII and VIII of Kendirya Vidyalaya, Surat;

3. The developed package was also field tested for the students of Government Sardar Vidyalaya, Churu (Rajasthan) which revealed it to be significantly effective in teaching these student as well as the students of KRS Visyalaya, Bareilly (UP) and also for the students of Classes VII and VIII of three states; and
5. The majority of the students liked and enjoyed learning through video-instructional package. They found it knowledgeable, innovative, systematic and interesting.

In the doctoral level experimentally study on "Effectiveness of audio-video intervention in developing listening comprehension in English at higher secondary stage (Bharathiar University) Ilangovan, K.N. (1988) tried:

1. to establish the relative effectiveness among the different instructional strategies, viz., Conventional Teaching Method (CTM), Media-based Non-interactive Group Instruction (MNGI) and AV presentation as a Support System (SS) in developing listening comprehension in English at higher secondary stage;
2. to find out whether there is significant difference among the different instructional strategies, viz., CTM, MNGI and AV as a support system (SS) in terms of their effectiveness in modifying the micro-skills which are required for local listening comprehension and global listening comprehension among the higher secondary students;
3. to develop syllabus based audio-video materials in developing listening comprehension in English among the students at the higher secondary stage;
4. to develop audio-video materials for testing and assessing the performance of the higher secondary students in listening comprehension in English before and after experimentation;

5. to evaluate the developed audio-video materials from technical and pedagogical points of view by experts, educationists and practicing teachers of English;
6. to find out whether there is any significant difference among different instructional strategies, viz., conventional teaching method (CTM), Media-based Non-interactive Group Instruction and AV presentation as support system in their effectiveness in terms of their retention of micro-skills required for local listening comprehension and global listening comprehension; and
7. to find out whether there is significant difference with regard to students' academic achievement in English before and after experimentation owing to the intervention of AV presentation in developing listening comprehension skills of the higher secondary students.

The experiment was tried on a sample of 105 students of Standard XI divided into three groups, one as control group and the other as experimental groups. It was found that:

1. the three instructional strategies, viz. CTM, MNGI and A VPSS were effective in modifying and developing the skills of local and global listening comprehension in English at the higher secondary stage;
2. the CTM, MNGI and AVPSS were more effective in developing all the micro-skills in respect of listening comprehension in English at the higher secondary stage;
3. the CTM, MNGI and AVPSS were different in their effectiveness while modifying the skills of local and global listening comprehension in English among students. AVPSS was the most effective instructional strategy as compared to others;

4. CTM, MNGI and AVPSS were more effective as compared to CTM in modifying in different micro-skills of the local and global listening comprehension in English among higher secondary students. But these were equally effective in modifying the micro-skills such as listening to contextual speech via picture cues and local listening comprehension via audio model;
5. it was found that the MNGI were more effective in comparison to CTM in modifying the micro-skills, i.e., listening to lecture and news items both, in audio-mode but they were equally effective in listening to modifying the listening to news item and listening to talk, both in video mode;
6. it was found that the MNGI were more effective when compared to AVPSS in modifying the micro-skills, i.e. listening to lectures via audio mode but AVPSS was more effective as compared to MNGI while listening to news item via video mode;
7. AVPSS was found more effective as compared to MNGI and CTM in enhancing the retention of the skills of listening comprehension and local listening comprehension, whereas MNGI was more effective as compared to CTM and AVPSS in enhancing retention of the skills of global listening comprehension among higher secondary students;
8. the MNGI was more effective as compared to CTM in enhancing retention on the skills of local listening comprehension namely the ability to discriminate among the distinctive vowels and consonants, to guess the meaning of the words listened to, to make use of real world knowledge and experience in understanding ideas and the ability to detect key words in English. While CTM was more effective as compared to MNGI on the skill of the ability to fix the related words in their proper contexts;

9. it was found that AVPSS was more effective as compared to MNGI and CTM in enhancing retention of the micro-skills namely the ability to detect attitude of speaker towards subject matter to identify relationship among units within discourse and the ability to make use of facial, paralinguistic and other clues to arrive at meaning; and
10. it was ascertained that the effectiveness of different instructional strategies differed from each other in realizing the instructional objectives in developing the listening skill and enhancing the retention of listening skills in English among higher secondary students.

Kothari, Saroi and Choudhary, Manju (1995) in their study on "Impact of television programme on behaviour of students of various age levels" tried to understand the effect of television programmes on students' emotional, creative, educational, moral and social behaviour on a sample of 150 students both boys and girls of Class VIII, X and XII selected at random revealed:

1. as regards the mean value of positive effect of television programmes on the children of all classes, girls had more positive effect on emotional and creative behaviour than boys. ON educational behaviour of Classes VIII and XII boys had more positive effect than girls. On moral behaviour and social behaviour, Class VIII and XII boys had more positive effect than girls, while Class X girls had more positive effect than boys;
2. as regards the mean value of negative effect of television programmes on children of all classes, Class VIII girls had more negative effect then boys. On creative behaviour Class VIII, X and XII girls had more negative effect than boys. On educational and moral behavior Class VIII and XII boys had

more negative effects than girls. On social behaviour, girls had more negative effect than boys;

3. Class XII boys had significant difference between positive and negative effect on emotional behaviour. On the basis of mean value of positive and negative effect on emotional behaviour of Class XII boys, television programmes had a more negative effect;
4. as regards the impact of television programmes on creative behaviour, in all classes, girls had a more positive effect of television programmes than boys but on the basis of mean value the negative effect was more on all students;
5. as regards the impact of television programmes on educational behaviour, there was no significant difference between the positive and negative effect on all students;
6. as regards the impact of television programmes on moral behaviour, the negative effect was more than the positive effect; and
7. as regards social behaviour, only Class X girls had significant difference between positive and negative effect while on the basis of mean value, television programmes had more positive effect on students social behaviour.

Mahajan, Sanjay, L. (1994) in a study on "Effectiveness of computer-assisted instructions for teaching singular and plural at II Grade attempted to establish the effectiveness of computer- assisted instructions (CAI) for teaching singular and plural at Grade II of two groups each made up of 20 Grade II students, matched on the basis of IQs. The tools used included paper-pencil tests and computer-assisted instructions. The study revealed that the CAI was more effective for teaching singular and plural as compared to traditional method.

Malik, J.S. (1993) in his doctoral research on "Technology transfer model: An analysis of linkages" (Choudhary Charan

Singh Haryana Agricultural University) sought to provide a deep insight into the functional linkages in the execution of the farmer's advisory services (FAS) of the Directorate of Extension Education, CCS HAU, Hissar at the state, district and the village (farmers) levels, besides the study of unshowing linkages with the field functionaries of the State Department of Agriculture, Government of Haryana in the transfer of the technology generated by the different subject matter departments of the constituent colleges. Its specific objectives are:

1. to study the university technology transfer mode in historical perspective;
2. to critically examine the interdepartmental linkages essential for reinforcing and revitalizing the technology transfer model;
3. to determine the adequacy of linkages within and outside the university for efficient feedback;
4. to make an assessment of farmers' perception of the technology transfer system of the university; and
5. to suggest medications in the existing extension model for quick transfer of technology.

It found that:

1. a significant majority of HODs (83.33%) had not obtained training in extension education;
2. half of the VLEs felt satisfied on the job of ULEs;
3. the field functionaries acknowledged both direct and indirect help from HAU for their professional enrichment;
4. a majority of the farmers who had been visiting KGKs were observed to be in low to medium age group; and
5. a significant majority of the farmers visiting KGKs demanded the required quantity of seed for demonstration plots.

Purushottaman, S. and Stella (1994) in "Effectiveness of teacher-controlled interactive video for group instruction" seeking to develop a teacher-controlled interactive video programme and to find it effectiveness, found that:

1. the teacher controlled IV technique resulted in better academic achievement compared to the other two techniques under study;
2. the indispensability of a teacher along with the innovative technique of video assisted learning;
3. the teacher's role when combined with a validated video lesson was able to produce the most desired effect on learning; and
4. the traditional question whether the teacher component would be eliminated from the system of education was emphatically denied or rules out from the findings.

This study was conducted on a sample of three random groups of 30, each consisting of teacher-trainees of secondary teacher education level. The script for the video lesson was prepared on the topic 'Psychology of learning'. The tools used were LV. treatment and traditional lecture-cum-discussion.

Sahoo, Namita and Goel, D.R. (1995) studied the UGC Countrywide classroom with and without talk-back with specific reference to higher education ETV programmes in terms of their contents, presentation and effectiveness. Out of the countrywide classroom ETV programmes telecast from September 1990 to January 1991, 10 programmes on social science were recorded fro the study. The purposive sampling technique was employed for selecting the student sample of 40 students of graduation level course of social science group belonging to School of Education, Devi Ahilya Vishwavidyalya, Indore admitted during 1990-91 academic session. It revealed:

1. as regards contents and presentation of CVCR programmes:
   (a) the sound and visuals were clear in most of the programmes, the colour choice was

appropriate. There was optimum coordination between the sound and the visuals. The visuals representation was well sequenced;

(b) the number of teaching points when seen against the time of the programme were adequate;

(c) the speed of presentation was quite suitable;

(d) the individual teaching points were discussed adequately;

(e) language was of student level, the level of the programme in relation to the grade was suitable;

(f) a large number of programmes were at understanding level;

(g) in some of the programmes there was indoor shooting whereas in the other it was indoor as well as outdoor;

(h) the background music and audio-visual ratio in most of the programmes could be improved.

2. in eight programmes out of ten, there was significant gain whereas in the two programmes there was no significant gain because the programmes were just solo talk, there were absolutely no visuals and the speed of delivery was relatively fast;

3. in eight programmes out of ten there was no significant difference between the mean scores of Hindi and English medium students;

4. there was no significant difference between the mean achievement of Native and Imported programmes;

5. the gain in three programmes out of ten was significant through the CWCR with talkback, whereas there was no significant difference in the achievement in the rest of the seven programmes with and without talkback; and

6. the viewers were found to have positive reactions towards CWCR programmes except towards adequacy of teaching point, appropriateness of language and pronunciation and skillful conduction of demonstration.

Sharma, Vashni (1995) In a study "On children's mass media communication" sought to analyse and interpret mass media communication of children that appeared in The Television Commercial Advertisements between 1991 and 1994 directed at children, of children by children and only for children employing content analysis in terms of both the channels: auditory and visual, problems in measurement, language and language-play, disclaimers, etc. Content analysis Technique was employed for analyzing the behavioural contents of commercial advertisements as well as of children, their problems of measurement, understandability and comprehensibility, language and language-play, semantics and syntax structures, linguistic capacity and competence of the children, disclaimers, etc. By and large, the paper encompasses the language used in various advertisements directed at children and mainly focuses on disclaimers and their intelligibility in young children. In addition to the content analysis of children's language dialogue and of commercial advertisements, as many as 17 main disclaimers were also analyzed, from the point of view of intelligibility and comprehensibility in young children. Analysis of semantics and syntactical structure from the points of view of linguistic competence among children constituted major determinants of communicability of the children. The study found that:

1. in the case of children's television advertising, the need to use colloquial language was even greater than it was in advertising directed at adults for fewer children used formal styles and because of its richer vocabulary, most young children encountered difficulties in understanding formal English/Hindi advertisement. This represent just one of the aspects in which children were disadvantaged linguistically;

2. language-play was an extraordinary common feature of such advertising;
3. Rhyme and alliteration were very commonly used;
4. the use of language play in children's television advertising was to amuse children and thus keep their attention;
5. as regards the disclaimers that appeared in children's television advertising that the question of the linguistic comprehension of children was most critical;
6. none of the disclaimers used, could be said to be colloquial in style and most of them presented problems for young children;
7. moreover disclaimers were extraordinarily elliptical material;
8. reconstruction of the elliptical was a more complicated process for the children to which they were addressed in these disclaimers;
9. language style were beyond the linguistic competence of most young children;
10. the most interesting linguistic advertising technique was the use of strong sounding but logically weak or empirically in determining language;
11. young children did not have full control over language and were not fully developed cognitively and as a result, failed to understand certain things advertisers said and would misunderstand others;
12. the disclaimers that were used were commonly in the passive voice, were highly elliptical and employed semantically complex words, such disclaimers had been proved to be unintelligible to young children.

Singh, Basant Bahadur (1994) m a study on "Effectiveness of U.G.C. countrywide classroom programmes on models of teaching with talk-back and with interactive mode" sought to find out the comparative effectiveness of the U.G.C. countrywide classroom programmes in terms of achievement of the viewers with interaction and with talk-back when pre-test scores were taken as a covariate. The study was conducted on B.Ed. students and it revealed:

1. the adjusted mean achievement on the test of group with talk-back and with interactive mode differed significantly; and
2. the interactive group was likely to perform significantly better than the group with talk-back.

Aggarwal, Y.P. and Mohanty, Manisha (1998) in a paper on "Effectiveness of Multi-media, Programmed Learning and Traditional Method of Teaching: A Meta Analytical Study of Indian Researchers" revealed that:

1. the performance of an average student either taught by Programmed learning method or Multi-media method was superior to that of student taught by Traditional method;
2. effect-size at Secondary level was found to be higher than that of primary level, that indicates that the modern method, i.e. PLM or MM is more effective for secondary level as compared to primary level;
3. PLM and MM are more suited for the teaching and study of science as compared to arts; and
4. in all comparisons of PLM vs TM and MM vs TM individually revealed that each of these innovative methods was superior to TM in overall situation.

In his doctoral study on "Development of Computer-based Time-space-personnel Management System" conducted on a sample of 54 University Teaching Departments/affiliated colleges, Institute of Education, Devi Ahilya Vishwavidyalaya and a Central School of Indore with its twenty eight teaching staff Biswal, Ashutosh (1995) revealed that:

1. the administrators did not find the manual time-table suitable to accommodate all curricular and

co-curricular activities and felt e need for a computer-based time-table in place of manually prepared time-table;

2. computer-based software to analyze time-space-personnel management system was effective to help administrators, teachers, TSPMS designers, students and visitors by creating different formats of TSPMS for different purposes which helped institutions to manage their available time, space and personnel effectively;
3. time-table generated through computer- based time-space- personnel- management system was effective in terms of suitable allotment of periods, even distribution of different periods and persons, time-tabling of co-curricular activities; and
4. the reaction of the teachers was positive and significant in different aspects towards the time-tables generated through computer.

Chetanlal, Neera (1899) in her experimental study "The Production of Validation of Video Teaching-learning Material in Home Science for Senior Secondary Students of Delhi" investigated:

1. the comparative efficacy of video teaching- learning material (VTLM), video-aided instruction (VAI) and conventional teaching (CT) in achievement of concepts in selected units of home science for Class XII students;
2. the attitude of students towards VLTMs.

She found that:

1. pre-test scores of the three groups belonging to three levels of intelligence and their interaction effects were not significant;
2. students exposed to video-teaching-learning material and video-aided instruction achieved higher as compared to conventional teaching;

3. video teaching-learning material and video-aided instruction were not significantly different;
4. the students having low intelligence achieved higher when exposed to video teaching-learning material as compared to video-aided instruction;
5. on retention test scores, significant differences were observed in three different treatments. Students exposed to video teaching learning material and video-aided instruction retained more concepts in home science as compared to conventional teaching;
6. students exposed to video teaching-learning material achieved higher as compared to video-aided instruction on retention test; and
7. majority of students had favourable attitude towards video teaching-learning material.

In a case study titled "Prospects and Problems in the Use of Educational Media: Case Study of an Agriculture University" Kumar, Niraj (1998) attempted to explore the problems experienced by the teachers in using media in their classroom teaching in the context of Agriculture Universities in India. The study was conducted on a randomly selected 104 teachers from six colleges located in the main campus of Govind Ballabh Pant University of Agriculture and Technology, Pantnagar. It revealed that:

1. majority of the teachers belonged to middle age group followed by young and old categories;
2. most of the teachers had doctorate and had experience of studying under new system and a considerable number of teachers had foreign exposure during their academic career;
3. maximum number of teachers had experience of less than 11 years in teaching and had served more than one organization;
4. by and large, teachers had considerably high professional orientation but they lacked training in instructional media;

5. most of the teachers had high favourable attitude towards instructional medial;
6. most of the teachers were highly aware of different instructional media but only a few felt that they had media-operating capability and media production capability;
7. the university had well-established media production and utilization system and its communication centre is well-equipped with required equipments, facilities and manpower, though while reacting on the problems faced, teachers ranked lack of own media production facilities as most important;
8. majority of the teachers were using only chalkboard as a teaching aid, charts and posters were other media used by about 79 percent of teachers but only in some classes, overall, the level of media utilization by teachers was very poor;
9. the main three problems ranked by most of the teachers were lack of own media production facilities followed by lack of financial support and availability of media.

In a doctoral study on "Newspapers as ELT Materials" Khan, R.A. (1996) explored the possibility of utilizing news items for all purposes with the specific objectives:

1. to emphasize the role of newspaper as teaching material;
2. to motivate teachers to look for text-free material; and
3. to provide initiative in adopting a new strategy of teaching English.

The study was conducted on a sample affiliated colleges of Vikarm University. A set of 20 lessons was prepared and tried in the classroom of the colleges covering areas of linguistic importance that equip learners with all necessary tools by which they could manipulate their acquired knowledge in whatever situations they were placed. It revealed that newspapers and journals were found motivating and appealing. The interest of the readers is sustained because of the variety of tastes they cater for and its novelty. The students are exposed to the current usage and not on an outdated model of language.

In short, newspapers make good materials if they are examined and viewed for their semantic, situational and communicative values. They not only motivate students but also induce the teachers to be ever on alert.

Conclusion and Observation

The review of recent studies on educational uses of television shows that television has been used to telecast programmes for higher education in the area of science and technology education in Western countries. Its effectiveness was studied in terms of programme contents, presentation, students' reactions and effectiveness. Both surveys and experimental methods were used. Relevant data were collected through questionnaires, interview schedules and tests.

The television in India has been used for educational purposes for almost last four decades. It started with school programmes at the secondary and senior secondary levels. Later it was extended to primary school level and higher education level. Experiments were undertaken to study the effectiveness of ETV programmes at the secondary and higher education level in terms of the content, quality of presentation, effectiveness and teachers' and students' attitude towards the ETV programmes.

The ETV programme entitled TARANG has been telecast for the last about a decade for the primary school children. However, no comprehensive study has been undertaken to study the status of the provision of need facilities for ETV programmes in schools. No study has also been conducted to study the nature and extend of utilisation of the available as well as needed facilities for ETV programmes specially at the primary stage. Impact and effectiveness studies need to be undertaken in relation to the content of the programmes, the quality of their presentation and learning achievement of students and their presentation and learning achievement of students and their reactions towards the ETV programme. More experimental studies than sample surveys need to be conducted to understand the psycho-social factors of classroom teaching-learning through use of television in education.

Experimental Study on Educational Television Programme in India on South Zone Delhi Primary Schools

Introduction

This chapter presents the method of research used, the design employed, sample selected, tools used, sequence of events that occurred, procedure adopted for data collection and statistical techniques used for analysis of data. After formulating the problem and reviewing related literature, it is worked out empirically so that valid and reliable solutions to the questions that the research poses can be obtained. This necessitates to select appropriate methodology of research.

The present study was conducted in two phases - first comprises the status study of utilization of ETV facilities in primary schools; second aimed at investigation into the effectiveness of the ETV programmes broadcast by Doordarshan. Therefore, the normative survey method was employed in the first phase and the experimental method in the second phase

Statement of the Problem

The problem for research may be stated in specific terms as follows:

A STUDY OF UTILISATION AND EFFECTIVENESS OF EDUCATIONAL TELEVISION (ETV) PROGRAMMES AT PRIMARY SCHOOL LEVEL

Definition of Key Terms

Utilization: The nature and extent to which the ETV Programmes are actually used in a school situation.

Effectiveness: The effect of a programme (here it is ETV Programme) in terms of the criterion which is an objective of the programme. Effectiveness of ETV programme means the gain in students learning of Math and EVS in classes III and V and change in learners' reaction towards ETV programmes.

Educational Television: The telecast of programmes for educational purposes on television set being provided in schools with a programme schedule.

Programmes: An organised body of educational activities or offerings like the syllabus based or general awareness topics with an achievable purpose.

Primary School Level: The stage of formal schooling generally starts at 6 years or first grade/class to 11 years or grade V. The primary schools offer organised sustained instruction designed to offer knowledge and skill in reading, writing and arithmetic along with awareness in environmental sciences - social as well as physical.

Achievement Test: An examination that seeks to test the extent to which a learner has acquired knowledge or skill, usually as a result of specific instruction or teaching programme.

Attitude Test: Attitude IS a disposition towards some phenomenon, idea, object or persons having cognitive, affective and evaluation aspects.

Attitude test is an examination designed to assess the attitude held by an individual or a group towards a particular phenomenon.

Objectives

Keeping in view the above stated problem, the main objectives of the study are stated as follows:

1. To conduct a survey of the effectiveness and utilisation of ETV programmes in Delhi at primary school level.
2. To study the effect of ETV programmes on primary school children class III and V in terms of their achievement of ETV lessons (EVS and Maths) and attitude towards ETV.
3. To study the effect of intervention programmes. Post telecast discussion to be conducted by teachers alongwith [L- L) ETV Programmes in primary school children in terms of their achievement of ETV lessons (EVS and Maths) and attitude towards ETV Programmes.
4. To study the attitude of class teachers towards quality of ETV programmes.
5. To make recommendations to planners and producers on different aspects of ETV Programmes.

Hypotheses

The following directional hypotheses are formulated keeping in view the objectives of the study:

1. Learners will utilize ETV programmes to great extent in Delhi at primary classes III and V.
2. Learners exposed to ETV programmes in schools will have, higher academic achievement than those who are not exposed to such programmes.
3. Learners exposed to ETV programmes In schools will show more favourable attitude towards ETV than those who are not exposed to such programmes.
4. Learners exposed to ETV programmes in schools along with intervention programmes will have higher academic achievement than those who are exposed to ETV programmes without intervention.
5. Learners exposed to ETV programmes in schools along with intervention programmes will show

more favourable attitude towards ETV than those who are exposed to ETV programmes without interventions.

6. Teachers will have positive attitude towards the quality of ETV programmes.

Delimitations of the Study

The study was confined to classes III and V and the class teachers of primary schools

Phase I: Normative Survey Method

Although, there are a wide variety of methods used in educational research, one's choice depends on the nature of problem. Here one of the objectives is to find out the availability of facilities for viewing educational television programmes and the extent of its utilization in primary schools in Delhi. Therefore, in fulfilling this objective the method employed in the study is normative survey. Some of the characteristics of the normative survey method of research are as follows:

1. It is essentially cross sectional, mostly of what exists type of status finding method.
2. It is concerned not with the characteristics of individuals but with generalized statistics of the whole population or the sampled thereof.
3. It requires an imaginative planning, careful analysis and interpretation of data and a logical and skillful reporting of the findings.
4. It does not aspire to develop an organised body of scientific laws. But provides information useful for generating hypotheses and solution of problems.
5. Surveys may be quantitative or qualitative in nature.
6. This is one of the methods of descriptive research. Description may be either verbal or expressed in mathematical symbols.

7. The information collected through questionnaires, interview schedules, etc. may include analytical studies of the data including descriptive presentation.
8. Standardized psychological tests can also be used for collecting required data for the normative survey.

Phase II: Experimental Method

Success of any research activity and its outcome depends essentially upon its research design. Kerlinger (1974) described, "Research design as the plan, structure and model of investigation conceived so as to obtain answers to research questions and control variance". Thus design provides a picture of what and how to do the research work. In any research project, design provides the investigator a blue print of research dictates the boundaries of the project and helps in controlling the experimental, extraneous and error variances of the problem under investigation.

The Design

In the present study (Phase-II), pre-test post-test control group design was employed in the experiment which was to be conducted in school without disturbing the school schedule. Therefore quasi-experimental research design was used. This design provides control of when and to whom the measurement is to arrange a situation in which the effects of variables can be investigated. Control eliminates the differential effects of all variables extraneous to the purpose of the study. The two groups (one experimental) and (a control) are naturally assembled groups as intact classes, which may be similar the subjects are not matched on previous learning achievement of knowledge about ETV lessons in Maths and ETV students for grade three and five of primary stage but equated (in mean and standard deviation) with respect to intelligence.

The design comprises one Experiment Group (El) which was taught through ETV lessons while the other Experimental

Group (E2) taught ETV lessons followed by teacher discussion. This treatment continued for about six weeks. Simultaneously the Control Group (G) was taught by the class teacher. All the three groups were given post-test in Math and EVS (SC and SS) to class ill students.

Same design was used in case of class V students who were also taught Math and EVS (SC and SS).

The experimental design of the study is given in Table 7.1.

Identification of Variables

In the experimental researches, the relationship between two types of variables namely independent and dependent variables is studied. Independent variables are the causes while dependent ones are the effects. Another category of variables, which is equally important, is intervening variable. All the three kinds of variables which were identified for the study are discussed below.

Independent Variables

There were two independent variables:

1. Teaching through ETV programmes to students of classes III and V.
2. Teaching through ETV programmes to students of classes III and V followed by post-telecast discussion by the teacher.

Dependent Variables

The following was taken as the main dependent variable:

Achievement of students of class III and V in the subjects of EVS (SC + SS) and Mathematics.

Intervening Variables

The main intervening variables considered in the experiment were:

1. Intelligence of the students.
2. Socio-economic Status (SES) of the students.
3. Class Teacher.
4. Type of school.

Table 7.1

Diagrammatic Representation of the Design

Stage	Duration	Experimental Group		Control Group	Lessons	
		E_1	E_2		Class III	Class V
Pre-test	One week	Administration of the following tests: • Intelligence test-Raven's Progressive Matrics • Achievement tests in EVS (SC+SS) and in Math • Students' reaction towards ETV			EVS	EVS
Treatment	Six weeks	Teaching by ETV lesson without post-telecast discussions	Teaching by ETV lessons + post-telecast discussion by the teacher	Conventional method of teaching EVS and Math	Math	Math
Post-Test	One week	Administration of the following tests: • Achievement tests in EVS (SC+SS) and in Math • Student's reaction towards ETV programme				

Controls Employed

It is necessary to control all those intervening variables that may affect the dependent variables. Hence suitable controls were applied for each such variable.

1. Intelligence of Students: This variable greatly influences the learning achievement of students. Therefore intelligence test using Raven's Progressive Matrices (Children Form) was administered and the two Experimental Groups - El and E2 and the Control Group - C were compared on mean and standard deviations. The three groups in the sampled schools for the experiment were found by and large equivalent.
2. Socio-economic Status (SES) of students: Since the students of primary school usually come from the same educational area and by and large similar SES level of the community and three groups (E_1, E_2 and C) were taken in the same school. It was assumed that the SES of students of primary schools is more or less of same level. Hence, no test of SES was given. Relevant statistical control was used to ensure the equivalence of the three groups (E_1, E_2 and C) in the same school selected for the experimental phase of the study.

The various types of variables with the control are shown in table 7.2.

Normative Survey of Utilization of ETV

The decision about research method guides the selection of the sample, variables to be considered, tools to be used for collection of data and statistical techniques to be applied for analysis of data. These are discussed in the following sections.

Selection of Sample

Most of the social, political and educational research problems involve selecting a representative sample. It is always desirable to select a smaller group from the whole population because it is economical both in time and effort.

Table 7.2
Summary of Independent, Dependent and Intervening Variables

Type of School	Grade/Class	Independent	Dependent	Intervening	Control
MCD Primary Schools (N=30)	III V	1. Teaching through ETV Lessons 2. Teaching through ETV lessons + Post-telecast Discussion	Achievement in EVS and Math	1. Intelligence 2. SES 3. Teacher 4. Type of Schools	Statistical Sampling Same Teacher Same type of school
KV Schools (N=6)	III V	1. Teaching through ETV Lessons 2. Teaching through ETV lessons + Post-telecast Discussion	Achievement in EVS and Math	1. Intelligence 2. SES 3. Teacher 4. Type of Schools	Statistical Sampling Same Teacher Same type of school
Directorate of Education (N=6)	–	–	–	–	–

Note: In the survey phase of the study, it was found that none of the primary sections of the Sarvodaya Vidyalayas (Sr. sec. Schools) under the Directorate of Education, Delhi which were included in the sample were utilizing ETV programmes for classes III V. Hence these schools were excluded in the experimental phase of the study.

Sometimes, it is impossible to cover the whole population however laborious and time consuming an attempt might be. Hence social scientists and statisticians have found out certain methods of getting a sample of adequate size and degree of representativeness of the population.

The Criteria for Selecting a Sampling Design

Young (1968) has suggested three criteria which should be kept in mind while constructing a sampling design.

1. A measurable or known probability sampling technique should be preferred so that risk of errors in the sample estimate can be controlled.
2. Simple, straight forward and workable methods adapted to available facilities and personnel should be used.
3. An attempt should be made to achieve maximum reliability of results for each dollar spent. Striking at an optimum balance between expenditures and a maximum of reliable information should be the guiding principle.

Population

"A population from statistical point of view is any arbitrarily defined group". Rarely would any statistical study regard the entire population of a nation, a city of some geographical region as its universe. The population in statistical investigation is always arbitrately defined by naming its unique properties.

In this study, the universe or population is comprised of all primary schools located in the National Capital Region of Delhi.

Sample

The term sample is defined as "a fraction of the population understudy which can represent the population in all the character and the results of the sample can be generalized to that of the whole population". A sample is said to be a miniature picture or replica of the whole population. A sample before it can be called true replica of the population, must fulfill at least two conditions. In the first place, it should be a "representative" one. It means that it must include all such possible characteristics of the population that divide it into mutually exclusive segments, such as males and females. Secondly, it must be "adequate". It means the adequate or sufficient size to allow confidence in the stability of its characteristics. All such procedure of sampling can be summed up under two halves "probability" and "non-probability" sampling procedures. Probability sampling means that each element of the population has an equal chance of being included in the sample. In such a sampling procedure, it is also possible to specify to extent to which the sample recruits might differ from population results. In addition to these, this is the only procedure which also guarantees the representativeness of the sample. The major forms of probability sampling are: simple random sample, stratified random sample and cluster sample. However, due to practical difficulties the investigator could not adopt stratified random sampling procedure and resorted to purposive sampling only.

Sampling Procedure

In the beginning the population statistics of the primary schools in Delhi was procured from the Directorate of Education, Delhi. The same is presented in table 7.3.

Table 7.3

Primary Schools under Different Managements in Delhi

Sl.No.	Type of Management	No. of Schools	Districts
1.	Municipal Corporation of	1840	278
2.	Delhi		
3.	Kendriya Vidyalayas	65	15
4.	Sarvodaya Vidyalayas	395	32
5.	Private Aided	202	27
6.	Private Unaided	1347	137
7.	Delhi Cantonment Board	8	–

Source: DISE (UEE Mission) Delhi as on 30.9.2002

Keeping in view the limited time and effort, the investigator decided to take the sample of the study from South Zone of Delhi. It was further decided to delimit the study only to:

1. MCD Primary Schools;
2. primary sections of the Kendriya Vidyalayas; and
3. Sarvodaya Vidyalayas under the Directorate of Education, Delhi.

In fact, it was found practically difficult to select schools strictly based on stratified sampling procedure. Therefore, investigator resorted to purposive sampling. The final sample selected for the study is presented in table 7.4.

Table 7.4

Sample of Primary Schools from South District of Delhi

Sl.No.	Type of Management	No. of Primary Schools	Delhi Zone
1.	M.C.D. Primary Schools	30	South
2.	K.V. Primary Sections	4	South
3.	Primary Sections of Sarvodaya Vidyalayas under Directorate of Education	6	South
	Total	40	

Development of Tools

The investigator developed the following tools specifically for collecting required data of this study:

1. Questionnaire for Headmasters and Teachers

A questionnaire was developed to study the nature and extent of utilization of Educational Television Programmes in Delhi schools. It has two sections. Section A on identification of data comprised 20 items while Section B on provision of facilities, knowledge about ETV programme nature and schedule and extent of utilization process of ETV programme comprised 23 main questions and sub-questions of some of the main questions. All answers and information required can be directly fed into the computer for analysis of the data.

2. Achievement Test for Class III in EVS and Mathematics

The objective was to assess 3rd class students learning achievement in EVS and Maths. The achievement test in EVS consisted of 48 multiple choice questions in Science and 30 questions in Social Studies. The achievement test in Mathematics comprised of 27 questions of multiple choice type.

3. Achievement Tests for Class V in EVS and Mathematics

The purpose was to evaluate 5th class students of learning achievement in EVS (Science + Social Studies) and Mathematics. The test consisted of 50 multiple choice questions in Science, 26 questions in Social Studies and 40 questions in Mathematics.

4. Teacher Attitude towards Educational Television (ETV) Programmes - A Rating Scale

The purpose of this scale is to assess teachers' attitude towards ETV programme. The scale consisted of 40 statements to be rated on a Likert type five-point scale.

Learner Reactions towards ETV Programmes - An Interview Schedule.

Procedure of Data Collection

The required data of the study were collected with the help of a questionnaire, achievement tests, attitude scales and interview schedule, etc. The procedure followed was as given below:

1. First of all a sample of primary schools under MCD were selected from South Zone of Delhi. It was followed by selection of only those senior secondary schools under Kendriya Vidyalaya Sangathan and Directorate of Education, Delhi which have primary sections attached to them.
2. Concerned educational authorities under MCD, KVS and DEO were requested to all the researcher to collect data relevant to provision and utilization of facilities for ETV programmes in the sampled schools.

3. Researcher visited the sampled schools with prior intimation to the schools, requested the Principals/ Headmasters to furnish information on ETV with the help of a questionnaire.
4. After getting the date and time for administering the tests in classes III and V, the researcher visited the sampled schools and collected the data as per the psychometric procedure.
5. The investigator then selected 3 MCD primary schoosl and 3 KVS senior secondary school for the experimental study. Treatments were given to the experimental schools for a period of six weeks. E_1 was viewing ETV and E_2 was viewing followed by discussion.
6. Post-test data were collected from experimental schools after the treatment was over. The data included learning achievement of III and V class students in Maths and EVS (SC and SS), attitude of teachers and reactions of students towards ETV programmes.

In all, the researcher had visited the sampled schools five times in connection with collection of data from Principal/ Headmasters, teachers and students of the primary schools under MCD and primary section of senior secondary schools under KVS and DEO, in South District of Delhi.

8

Analysis and Interpretation

Introduction

This chapter presents the tabulation and analysis of data obtained both at the survey and experimental stages of the study. The data are subjected to statistical analysis so that the valid and reliable conclusions about the sample and the experimental treatment can be drawn.

It has been mentioned earlier that the present study involves two stages - survey and experiment. The aim of conducting survey is to study the status of provision of facilities available in primary schools of South Zone of Delhi for ETV programme and the knowledge and utilisation of the facilities by teachers and headmasters for effective use of ETV for student learning. The experimental part of the study aims at studying the effectiveness of ETV in terms of students' achievement in mathematics and environmental studies (EVS - SC and SS), also attitude of students and teachers towards ETV programmes of classes III and V.

Educational Television Programme in Schools – A Survey

The survey of the facilities included aspects such as provision of TV sets, place and duration of viewing, conditions of viewing, teachers' knowledge about ETV programmes - their purpose and source, the schedule, channel, etc. Besides problems and issues in providing necessary facilities for effective utilisation of the ETV programmes. The results of the data collected on these aspects according to the types of school are presented in this section.

Status of ETV Facilities

(a) Schools with TV Sets and Viewing Facilities

Schools taken for the study are from MCD, Kendriya Vidyalayas and Directorate of Education. Number of schools are 40; 30 from MCD, 4 from Kendriya Vidyalayas and 6 from DEO.

Table 8.1

Number of Schools with Educational Television Sets, Place of Viewing - how long Available, etc.

Sl.No.	Status	Type of School		
		MCD (N=30)	KV (N = 4)	DOE (N=6)
1.	TV sets are available or not			
	Yes	22	3	2
	No	8	1	4
2.	How long available?			
	(a) Less than 5 years	–	–	–
	(b) 5-10 years	4	–	–
	(c) 10 years or more	18	3	2
3.	Functional Status			
	(a) Function regularly	6	2	–
	(b) Function Occasionally	8	1	1
	(c) Does not function most of the time	6	–	–
	(d) Does not function at all	2	–	1
4.	Place of viewing			
	(a) Separate room	2	3	–
	(b) Classroom	–	–	–
	(c) Sports room	1	–	–
	(d) Headmaster's room	18	–	1
	(e) Teachers' staff room	1	–	1

Availability of Television sets is different in all types of schools. Just as many as 22 sets are present in 30 MCD schools, 3 sets in Kendriya Vidyalayas and 2 in DOE schools have the same. So MCD schools and Kendriya Vidyalayas are in better position because 73.33% schools of MCD schools and 75% Kendriya Vidyalayas are having television sets whereas only 33.33% schools of DOE are having television sets.

One of the major factors of DOE schools not having television set is that primary section of senior secondary schools is neglected. The principal pays much attention only to tenth and twelfth classes. On the other hand there is no post of a headmaster in primary section, but is only incharge looks after primary classes. There is no proper arrangement of television set and facilities related to it.

In 18 schools of MCD, 3 Kendriya Vidyalayas and 2 schools of DOE, television sets are available for the last more than 10 years. In 4 schools of MCD television sets are available for less than 10 years. But there is a question mark on their functioning. In 6 MCD schools and 2 Kendriya Vidyalayas television sets are functioning regularly, while in 8 MCD schools, 1 Kendriya Vidyalaya and 1 DOE school television sets are functioning occasionally. On the other hand, in 6 MCD schools they do not function most of the time, whereas in 2 MCD schools and in 1 DOE school, they do not function at all. This shows that functional status of TV sets is better in MDC schools and Kendriya Vidyalayas than schools under DOE.

Place of viewing TV is also a problem in many schools. Only 2 MCD schools are having separate ETV room where they view the programme. However in 18 schools of MCD, television is placed in Headmaster's room and in one school it is placed in teachers' staff room. In all the three Kendriya Vidyalayas in which television sets are available are having separate ETV rooms. Only one DOE school, it is placed in Headmaster's room while in the school, it is placed in teachers' staff room. The data shows that there is a need for separate ETV room for viewing television in schools.

(b) Viewing Condition and Functionality of TV sets

The status regarding viewing conditions and its information conveyed to the higher authorities in case of television sets being out of order or needed replacement is presented in table 8.2.

Table 8.2

Sl.No.	Status	Type of School		
		MCD (N=30)	KV (N = 4)	DOE (N=6)
1.	Viewing Conditions			
	(a) Satisfied	9	2	–
	(b) Not satisfied	13	1	2
2.	If 'no', reasons for non satisfaction			
	(a) Small rooms			
	(b) Noisy environment	2	1	–
	(c) Small size of TV set	1	–	–
	(d) Electric supply erratic	–	–	–
	(e) Other suggestions for improving	2	1	2
	(f) Viewing place should be separate	8	1	2
	(g) Particular teacher should operate ETV programme	1	1	–
3.	Informed higher authorities			
	Yes	13	3	1
	No	9	–	1
	How many days do they take to repair			
	(a) One week	1	1	–
	(b) One month	6	1	–
	(c) One year	1	–	–
	(d) No fixed time	5	1	–
	Reasons, if not informed			
	(a) No right response	5	–	1
	(b) Again TV set got out of order	4	–	–

It is observed that out of 30 MCD schools, only nine schools are having satisfactory viewing conditions while in

13 schools viewing conditions are not satisfactory. 2 Kendriya Vidyalayas are having satisfactory viewing condition and one is having unsatisfactory condition. However, in both the schools under DOE, viewing conditions are unsatisfactory. In terms of viewing conditions of Kendriya Vidyalayas and MCD schools are in better position. In case of unsatisfactory condition, 2 MCD schools have the problem of small rooms, 1 of noisy environment, 2 of erratic electric supply. However one Kendriya Vidyalaya has problem of small school and one has erratic electric supply. Both schools of DOE are having problems of erratic electric supply. Most of the schools gave valuable suggestions to overcome such situations. The teachers and Headmasters of 8 MCD, 1 Kendriya Vidyalaya and 2 DOE schools suggested that television viewing place should be separate. Teachers suggested that they can make a suitable time table and discuss the matter before the telecast. Besides, some teachers suggested that particular teacher trained in ETV, should be appointed for the programme.

As many as 13MCDschools out of 30 schools informed to their higher authorities about the malfunctioning of TV sets. Similarly three Kendriya Vidyalayas and one DOE school also informed to their higher authorities but nine MCD schools and one DOE school did not inform to their authorities because most of the time they do not get satisfactory response from concerned authorities. Generally it takes about minimum two months or sometimes more, even one year when authorities take note of the complaints about malfunctioning of TV sets.

(c) Knowledge of Channel and Programmes

Infrastructural facilities for ETV In schools are necessary. Also teachers' knowledge about the schedule of broadcast and sources of other relevant information is essential for making ETV purposeful and effective.

Table 8.3
Teachers' Knowledge about the ETV programmes and the Channel and Sources of Information

Sl.No.	Status	Type of School		
		MCD (N=30)	KV (N = 4)	DOE (N=6)
1.	ETV Programmes are being telecast at			
	(a) National Channel			
	Yes	21	3	2
	No	1	No TV	No TV
	(b) Gyan Darshan			
	Yes	15	–	–
	No	7	–	–
	Timings for telecast of ETV programmes			
	(a) 10.30 a.m. to 11.00 a.m. for Primary Stage	22	3	2
	(b) 10.30 a.m. to 11.00 a.m. for Secondary Stage	–	–	–
	(c) 10.30 a.m. to 11.00 a.m. for Teacher Education	–	–	–
2.	Which Channel is used National (DD-I)			
	Yes	21	3	2
	No	1	–	–
	If 'no', what is the reason(s) Not aware about TARANG Programme	–	1	–
3.	TV programmes being telecast, they come to know through			
	– News papers	3	–	–
	– TV	1	–	–
	– Education Officer	17	3	2
	– Parents	1	–	–

The status regarding knowledge of teachers about ETV programmes and the channels through which the television programmes are being telecast are shown in table 8.3. This table also shows sources of knowledge of ETV programmes. The data reveals that 21 MCD schools, all the three Kendriya Vidyalayas and two DOE schools are aware that National Channel (DD) telecast the ETV programmes whereas only one MCD is not aware about this fact. 15 out of 22 schools of MCD are aware about Gyan Darshan and 7 are not. Moreover, in Kendriya Vidyalayas and DOE schools they are not aware about Gyan Darshan channel of ETV programmes. Pertaining to the timings of the programme, all the three types of schools are using the same telecast time, i.e., 10.30 a.m. to 11.00 a.m. and watch only primary level programmes. Only DD-1 National Channel is the prime choice of all the three types of schools. One MCD school is not aware about TARANG programme. Majority of schools get the information about ETV programmes through their Education Officers. 17 out of 22 and all three Kendriya Vidyalayas and both the DOE schools get information through their Education Officers. However, three MCD schools get information through newspapers, one through television and another one through parents.

Purposes of ETV

The purposes of television sets being used in schools; whether teaches are having copy of ETV programme schedule and the presence of teachers during ETV programme, etc. are given in table 8.4.

Majority of the schools are using the television sets to view the ETV programmes. Only one MCD school use television for news and three for video shows of educational films. Regarding ETV programme schedule, 17 out of 22 MCD schools and 2 out of 3 Kendriya Vidyalayas are having the copies of ETV programme schedule, while 5 MCD schools, one Kendriya Vidyalayas and both the schools of DOE do not possess the programme schedules.

Table 8.4

Purpose of Television programme, ETV Programme Schedule and Teacher Presence during Telecast

Sl.No.	Status	Type of School		
		MCD (N=30)	KV (N = 4)	DOE (N=6)
1.	For what purpose the TV set is being used			
	(a) Viewing ETV programmes	22	3	2
	(b) News	1	–	–
	(c) Sports and games	–	–	–
	(d) Entertainment	–	–	–
	(e) Video shows of educational films	3	–	–
	(f) Any other	–	–	–
2.	Do the teachers have a copy of ETV programmes schedule			
	Yes	17	2	–
	No	5	1	2
	Did not give Education Officer	3	–	–
3.	Do the students watch the Educational TV programmes in presence of the teachers			
	(a) Always	11	2	–
	(b) Sometimes	10	1	1
	(c) Never	1	1	–

Students of 11 out of 22 MCD schools and 2 out of 3 Kendriya Vidyalayas view the ETV programmes always in presence of the teachers. Students of 10 MCD schools, 1 Kendriya Vidyalayas and 1 DOE schools view the ETV programmes sometimes in presence of the teachers. Students of one MCD and one DOE school view the ETV programmes without the presence of any teacher. This shows lack of interest of the teachers and need for curriculum based programmes to be telecast under ETV. Teachers should not only be present during ETV programme but should actively participate in pre and post telecast sessions.

Gyan Darshan Channel

In response to the question whether there is any specific period for ETV programme or not, it is found that 50% MCD schools and 100% Kendriya Vidyalayas are having separate period of ETV programmes. Remaining 50% of MCD and both the schools of DOE are not having separate period of ETV programmes. MCD schools reveal that most of the time there is no provision in the time table received from the Education Officers. Same is true at the schools under DOE. Other factors for not having a period of ETV are that these programmes are not integrated part of curriculum. They are not curriculum based. However, the TARANG programmes are in accordance with the syllabus.

Table 8.5

ETV programme in the School Time Table, use of Gyan Darshan Channel and Suitability of the Programme

Sl.No.	Status	Type of School		
		MCD (N=30)	KV (N = 4)	DOE (N=6)
1	2	3	4	5
1.	There is a period of ETV programme or not			
	Yes	11	3	–
	No	11	1	2
	(a) ETV programmes are not integrated in curriculum	3	1	–
	(b) Educational TV programmes are not curriculum bound	1	1	–
	(c) No provision in the time table received from EOS	7	1	2
2.	Do the Headmaster/teachers see Gyan Darshan Channels or not			
	Yes	–	–	–
	No	22	3	2
	Reason-Because Tarang programme in on DD-1	22	3	2

(Table Contd...)

1	2	3	4	5
3.	How do the teachers and headmasters decided the suitability of ETV programmes for the particular class and age group			
	(a) Programme Schedule	14	–	–
	(b) Content of the programme	1	–	–
	(c) Fixed days for specific class	7	–	2
	(d) Weekly programme highlights	–	–	–
	(e) Any other	–	–	–

The second problem is that of language because in Kendriya Vidyalayas books of science and mathematics are in English, whereas the ETV programme is telecast in Hindi. This is the major problem for students of Kendriya Vidyalayas.

Regarding the suitability of ETV programmes for particular class and age group, 22 MCD schools ETV programmes the children are according to the schedule and one MCD school according to the content, while 7 MCD schools, 3 Kendriya Vidyalayas and 2 DOE schools show ETV programmes to the children on fixed days for specific class.

Effective Utilization of ETV Programme

The data in Table 8.6 shows that there is a need of students' presence in the room before five minutes of ETV programme telecast. Three schools of MCD point out that proper seating arrangement is possible if students come to the TV room five minutes before and another three school teachers say that for checking the work of students, it is necessary to come to the viewing room five minutes before the telecast. Teachers of other three schools of MCD and Kendriya Vidyalayas say that student become ready for viewing the programme. However, majority of the schools, i.e. 13 out of 22 MCD schools, 1 out of 3 of Kendriya Vidyalayas and both the DOE schools say that they properly conduct pre-telecast discussion.

(d) Viewers and Teacher Factors

On the other hand some Headmasters say that there is no need for viewers to be present before 5 minutes because previous class teacher does not allow the class before five minutes. Seven out of 22 MCD schools respond in this manner and majority, i.e. 13 out of 22 MCD schools, all the three Kendriya Vidyalayas and both the DOE schools pointed out that ETV programmes do not match with the school time table.

Table 8.6

Viewer and Teacher Factors of Effective Utilization of ETV Programme

Sl. No.	Status	Type of School		
		MCD (N=30)	KV (N = 4)	DOE (N=6)
1.	Need of students presence before 5 minutes of ETV programme telecast			
	(a) Proper seating possible	3	–	–
	(b) Checking the work of ETV	3	–	–
	(c) Students become ready for viewing	3	2	–
	(d) Properly conduct pre-telecast discussion	13	1	2
	(e) Any other reasons	–	–	–
2.	Why there is no need to be present before 5 minutes			
	(a) Previous lesson not completed	–	–	–
	(b) Previous class teacher not allowed	7	–	–
	(c) ETV programme do not match with the school time-table	15	3	2
3.	Whether the teachers get training for effective utilization of ETV programmes			
	Yes	18	3	1
	No	4	–	1

The teachers of 18 MDC schools, all the Kendriya Vidyalayas and only one DOE school got training for effective utilization of ETV programmes. However 4 MDC schools and only one DOE school did not get training for better utilization of ETV programmes.

(e) Support of Education Officers

The visit-cum-discussion of Education Officers with the headmasters and teaches go a long way in making the ETV programme functional and effective. The following table presents data in respect of visit of Education Officers and headmasters discussion regarding problems of viewing of ETV programmes.

Table 8.7

Education Officer's visit and Discussion with Headmasters and Teachers

Sl.No.	Status	Type of School		
		MCD (N=30)	KV (N = 4)	DOE (N=6)
1	2	3	4	5
1.	How often the Education Officers visit the school			
	(a) Weekly	1	–	–
	(b) Monthly	17	1	2
	(c) Quarterly	4	2	–
	(d) Half yearly	–	–	–
	(e) Yearly	–	–	–
2.	Do the Headmaster and teachers discuss the problem with E.O.			
	(a) Educational Time-table			
	Yes	20	3	1
	No	2	–	1
	(b) Maintenance of TV set			
	Yes	17	3	–
	No	5	–	1
	(c) Programme schedule of Educational Television			
	Yes	18	3	–
	No	4	–	1

(Table Contd...)

1	2	3	4	5
	(d) Record register of ETV programme			
	Yes	9	2	–
	No	13	–	1
	(e) Telecast timings			
	Yes	9	2	–
	No	13	–	–
	(f) Viewing facilities			
	Yes	7	–	–
	No	15	–	–

The visit by Education Officers has been monthly to majority of schools of all the three types. In some MCD schools and 2 Kendriya Vidyalayas, Education Officers visit quarterly. Education Officers are generally overlook the facilities available for ETV viewing and it's utility. There should be a proper cooperation and support of Education Officers to maintenance of television and related problems. Headmasters of all the three types of schools discuss the problems of their schools with Education Officers. They discuss about the school time-table, maintenance of television sets and programme schedule of ETV programmes. In addition to these problems, all types of schools also discuss about record register of ETV programmes, telecast timings, viewing facilities, etc. Headmasters of MCD schools and Kendriya Vidyalayas are more serious to discuss their problems with the higher authorities.

(f) Utilisatin of ETV and Related Problems

Problems received from all types of school pertaining to effective utilization of ETV programmes (Table 8.8) include mechanical disorder of television sets, failure of electricity, lack of teachers' interest and telecast of unscheduled programmes, etc. Poor quality of ETV programmes leading to inattentiveness of pupils in viewing also affected the utility of ETV programmes adversely in MCD schools and Kendriya Vidyalayas. Lack of interest on the part of students of MCD schools is also a reason for effectiveness. Most of the teachers of MCD schools think that if they view ETV programmes it is waste of their time. It will not be helpful in completing the curriculum. The problems of repetition of the programmes and lack of security of television set also exist. Sometimes programmes are cut abruptly and complete programmes as per schedule are not telecast. These are some common factors behind less effectiveness of ETV in MCD schools.

Table 8.8

Problems of Headmaster and Teachers in respect of Effective Utilization of ETV programmes

Sl.No.	Status	Type of School		
		MCD (N=30)	KV (N = 4)	DOE (N=6)
1	2	3	4	5
1.	Mechanical disorder of Television sets			
	Yes	21	2	1
	No	1	1	–
2.	Failure of electricity			
	Yes	19	3	–
	No	3	1	–
3.	Bad wiring			
	Yes	3	–	–
	No	19	–	1
4.	Lack of space in the class			
	Yes	3	–	–
	No	19	–	–
5.	Poor quality of ETV programme			
	Yes	–	1	–
	No	22	2	–
6.	Lack of interest on the part of students			
	Yes	1	–	–
	No	21	–	–

(Table Contd...)

1	2	3	4	5
7.	Lack of interest on the part of the teachers			
	Yes	6	1	–
	No	16	2	–
8.	Repetition of programmes			
	Yes	4	1	–
	No	18	2	–
9.	Security of TV set			
	Yes	3	–	–
	No	18	2	–
10.	Programmes are cut abruptly			
	Yes	1	–	–
	No	21	–	–
11.	Complete programme as per schedule not telecast			
	Yes	4	–	–
	No	18	–	–

(g) Effects of Discussion

The data related to the affect of conducting pre-telecast and post-telecast discussion shows that Headmasters and teachers of all the three types of schools are in favour of pre-telecast discussion because it makes the content clear to the students and creates interest among the students for viewing the programmes. Through the telecast discussion, they can achieve more. It can motivate the children for the programmes and to learn from it more effectively.

Post-telecast discussion also affects the learning achievement and the learner both. Majority of MCD schools expressed that through post-telecast discussion, concepts become clear and difficult concept becomes more clear to the students. Post-telecast discussion reinforces the students' learning and gain from the EN programmes. Headmasters and teachers of all the three types of schools agree about post-telecast discussion which works as reinforced technique.

Teachers and Headmasters of some schools agree that repetition of the programmes make more and more clear to the children about the contents.

Table 8.9

Effects of Conducting Pre-telecast and Post-telecast Discussions

Sl.No.	Status	Type of School		
		MCD (N=30)	KV (N=4)	DOE (N=6)
1.	What are the effects of pre-telecast discussions			
	(a) Creating interest			
	Yes	21	3	2
	No	1	–	–
	Develop curiosity for receptions of ETV programmes			
	Yes	21	3	2
	No	1	–	–
	To make clear about the content	8	2	2
2.	What are the effects of conducting post-discussion			
	(a) Clarity of difficult concepts			
	Yes	21	–	–
	No	1	–	–
	Reinforce the learning gained in the programme			
	Yes	20	3	2
	No	2	–	–

There are certain positive effects on viewers learning due to effective utilization of ETV programmes. The Headmasters and teachers of M CD schools and all the three Kendriya Vidyalayas and one school of DOE feel that ETV helped in increasing the enrolment. However, 14 MCD schools, one school of DOE do not feel so. Improvement of attendance was possible only in 9 MCD and one ODE schools only. School dropout reduced in all three Kendriya Vidyalayas, one DOE and four MCD schools. Enrichment of learning is the key aspect in all three types of schools but Kendriya Vidyalayas and DOE schools are in better position than MCD schools in this aspect. Developing critical and creative thinking and developing scientific temper as positive effects of ETV was told by all the Kendriya Vidyalayas, DOE schools and 60% in MCD schools. Effective utilization plays an important role in developing positive attitude towards media in all the three types of schools. Media play an important role in embedding social values, feeling of cooperation among the students, but punctuality and regularity could not make such kind of difference.

Table 8.10

Positive Effects on Viewers Learning

Sl.No.	Status	Type of School		
		MCD (N=30)	KV (N=4)	DOE (N=6)
1	2	3	4	5
1.	(a) Positive effects on viewers learning			
	(b) Increase enrolment			
	Yes	8	3	1
	No	14	–	1
	(c) Improve attendance			
	Yes	9	–	1
	No	13	3	1
	(d) Reduce school dropout			
	Yes	4	3	1
	No	13	–	1
	(e) Enrichment of learning			
	Yes	12	3	2
	No	10	–	1
	(f) Develop critical and creative thinking			
	Yes	13	3	2
	No	9	–	–
	(g) Develop scientific temperament			
	Yes	13	3	2
	No	9	–	–

(Table Contd...)

1	2	3	4	5
	(h) Develop positive attitude towards media (credibility of media)			
	Yes	12	1	2
	No	10	2	–
	(i) Imbibe social values			
	Cooperation			
	Yes	12	1	2
	No	14	–	1
	Punctuality			
	Yes	7	–	1
	No	15	3	1
	Regularity			
	Yes	7	1	1
	No	15	2	1

(h) Suggestions

Suggestions from Headmasters and teachers were obtained for effective utilization of ETV programmes in primary schools for students' development and learning.

Several valuable suggestions for making effective utilization of ETV programmes in schools were made. By and large all the three types of schools say that there should be fixed time-table, suitable accommodation, more curriculum-based topics be covered by ETV programmes. Motivation and awareness should be generated among the viewers. There should be initiative by school Headmasters and Education Officers. Separate ETV period should be provided in the school time-table. There should be separate channel for ETV programmes and these should be life oriented. Wide publicity is needed for ETV programmes which should be curriculum based.

Headmasters and teaches view that ETV programmes are helpful for the students learning. It needs some useful changes. Material and facility related to the ETV programmes should be provided to the schools in a satisfactory way to make it more and more effective. Most part of the programmes should be life oriented so that learning may be helpful in life. Most of the teachers and learners are not aware about the utility of programmes, so there should be publicity of the programme and it should be curriculum based so that teacher and learner are motivated to view the ETV programmes in schools.

Table 8.11

Suggestion for Effective Utilization of ETV Programmes

Sl.No.	Status	Type of School		
		MCD (N=30)	KV (N=4)	DOE (N=6)
1	2	3	4	5
1.	Suitable time-table should be fixed			
	Yes	22	3	2
	No	–	–	–
2.	Suitable accommodation should be provided			
	Yes	22	3	2
	No	–	–	–
3.	More curriculum based topics to be covered by ETV programmes			
	Yes	22	3	2
	No	–	–	–
4.	Motivation and awareness should be generated among the viewers			
	Yes	22	3	2
	No	–	–	–
5.	Initiative of Headmaster of the school			
	Yes	20	3	2
	No	2	–	–
6.	Initiative of the Education Officer			
	Yes	18	3	2
	No	4	–	–
7.	Separate ETV period should be provided in the school time-table			
	Yes	20	3	2
	No	2	–	–

(Table Contd...)

1	2	3	4	5
8.	Separate channel for ETV programmes			
	Yes	21	3	2
	No	1	–	–
9.	ETV programmes should belief oriented			
	Yes	13	–	2
	No	9	–	–
10.	Wide publicity of ETV programmes			
	Yes	13	3	2
	No	9	–	–
11.	Programme should be curriculum based			
	Yes	8	–	2
	No	–	–	–

(i) Supply of Support Material

Table 8.12 presents the status of supply of support materials in schools. 50% of MCD schools, 100% of Kendriya Vidyalayas and 50% of DOE schools get the programme schedule. 50% of MCD schools and 66% of Kendriya Vidyalayas have teachers' guidelines. 50% of MCD schools and 100% of Kendriya Vidyalayas are having instructional material for use of teachers. Similarly 100% of Kendriya Vidyalayas and more than 54% of MCD schools have monthly ETV report register, monitoring schedule and observation schedule, but in DOE schools, anyone of the item is not available except programme schedule which is available in one school only.

Kendriya Vidyalayas are serious in having programme schedule, instructional material and maintaining the register. Although a majority of MCD schools are having all these documents and materials but register maintenance is not proper. The DOE schools are not having the supply of materials. The reasons may be that primary sections of DOE schools are generally ignored by the concerned authority with regard to viewing ETV programmes.

Table 8.12

Supply of Support Material

Sl.No.	Status	Type of School		
		MCD (N=30)	KV (N=4)	DOE (N=6)
1.	Programme schedule			
	Yes	11	3	1
	No	11		
2.	Teachers guidelines			
	Yes	13	2	
	No	9	1	2
3.	Instructional material for user teachers			
	Yes	11	3	–
	No	11	–	2
4.	Monthly ETV report from register			
	Yes	14	3	–
	No	8	–	2
5.	Monitoring schedule			
	Yes	13	3	–
	No	9	–	2
6.	Observation schedule			
	Yes	12	3	–
	No	10	–	2

Effectiveness of ETV Programmes - An Experimental Study

The objective of the experimental study is to assess the effectiveness of ETV programme in terms of students achievement in Math and EVS (SC + SS), attitude of teachers and learner reactions towards ETV programme of classes III and V.

Analysis of data has been done by using ANOVA to find out the significance of mean differences on pre-test of various groups on Math and EVS of classes III and V. 't' values were calculated to find out the significance of mean gain scores between three groups - E_1, E_2 and Control Group on Math and EVS for classes III and IV.

Analysis of data pertaining to teachers' attitude was analysed and 't' values were done to find out the significance of mean difference of attitude scores between three groups - E_I, E_s and Control Groups.

Analysis of Data of Experimental Study

Significance of mean differences on pre-test scores of various groups on Math and EVS of class III

From Table 8.13, the calculated value of F is 1.78 of pre-test scores of Math of Class Ill. This F value is less than the table value at .05 level. It indicates that pre-test scores of all the three groups – E_I, E_S, and Control Group do not differ significantly. Similarly the calculated value of F Value is 1.01 of pre-test scores of EVS of class III. This is less than the table value at .05 level. It indicates the pre-test scores of all the three groups - E_I, E_S, and Control Group do not differ significantly.

Table 8.13

Summary of ANOVA of Pre-test, Post-test and Gain Scores of Math and EVS of Class III

Subject	Stage		Sum of Squares	df	Mean	F	Sig.
1	2		3	4	5	6	7
Mathematics	Pre-test	Between Groups	28.950	2	14.475	1.784	.172
		Within Groups	949.175	117	8.113		
		Total	978.125	119			
	Post-test	Between Groups	367.850	2	183.925	18.708	.000
		Within Groups	1150.275	117	9.831		
		Total	1518.125	119			
	Gain	Between Groups	276.200	2	138.100	30.241	.000
		Within Groups	534.300	117	4.567		
		Total	810.500	119			

(Table Contd...)

1	2		3	4	5	6	7
EVS	Pre-test	Between Groups	67.267	2	33.633	1.011	.367
		Within Groups	3893.325	117	33.276		
		Total	3960.592	119			
	Post-test	Between Groups	2164.717	2	1082.358	21.734	.000
		Within Groups	5826.750	117	49.801		
		Total	7991.467	119			
	Gain	Between Groups	2258.150	2	1129.075	43.526	.000
		Within Groups	3034.975	117	25.940		
		Total	5293.-125	119			

From Table 8.13 the calculated value of F is 18.70 of post-test scores of Maths of class III. The F value is higher than the table value of Fat .01 level. It indicates that post-test scores of all groups - E_1, E_2 and CG differ significantly.

It is further seen that F is 21.73 of post-test scores of EVS of class Ill. The F value is higher than the table value of F at .01 level. It indicates that post-test scores of all groups - E_1, E_2 and CG differ significantly.

From Table 8.13, the calculated value of F is 301.24 of post-test gain scores of Math of class Ill. The value is higher than the table value of F at .01 level. It indicates that all post-test gain scores of all groups differ significantly. Similarly it is seen that calculated value of F is 43.53 of post-test gain scores of EVS of class III. The F value is higher than the table value of F at .01 level. It indicates that all post-test gain scores of all groups differ significantly.

The 't' Values of significance of Mean Gain Scores Between three Groups on Math of Class III

Table 8.14 shows that 't' value is 5.11 which is significant at .01 level with df 78. It indicates that the mean gain score of E_1, E_2 and CG of Math of class III differ significantly. Further the mean gain score of E_1 is 4.45 that is significantly higher than mean gain score of control group which is 2.30.

Table 8.14

Mean, SD and 't' Values of Mean Gain Difference between Various groups in EVS of Class III

		Group	M	SD	N	t-value	Remark
Math	Gain Score	E_1	4.45	2.35	40	5.11	Significant at 0.01 level
		Control Group	2.30	1.24	40		
		E_2	6.00	1.24	40	8.19	Significant at 0.01 level
		Control Group	2.30	2.57	40		
		E_1	4.45	1.24	40	2.81	Significant at 0.01 level
		E_2	6.00	2.35	40		

The table also shows that 't' value between E_2 and CG is 8.19 which is significant at .01 level with df 78. It indicates that mean gain score of E_2 and CG is Math of class III differ significantly. Further the mean gain score of E_2 is 6 or which is significantly higher than mean gain score of control group which is 2.30.

It is further seen that 't' value between E_1 and E_2 is 2.81 which is significant at .01 level with df 78. It indicates that mean gain score of E_1 and E_2 of Math of class III differ significantly. Further the mean gain score of E_2 is 6.00 that is significantly higher than mean gain score of El which is 4.45.

't' Values of Significance of Mean Gain Scores Between three Groups on EVS of Class III

Table 8.15 shows that 't' value 6.2 which is significant at 0.01 level with df 78. It indicates that mean gain score of E_1 and CG of EVS of class III differ significantly. Further mean gain score of E_1 is 9.80 which is higher than mean gain score of control group which is 4.80.

Table 8.15
Mean, SD and 't' Values of Mean Gain Difference between Various Groups in EVS of Class III

		Group	M	SD	N	t-value	Remark
EVS	Gain score	E_1	9.80	4.87	40	6.22	Significant at 0.01 level
		Control Group	4.60	2.07	40		
		E_2	15.23	7.05		9.14	Significant at 0.01 level
		Control Group	4.60	2.07			
		E_1	9.80	4.87		4.00	Significant at 0.01 level
		E_2	15.23	7.05			

The table further shows that 't' value between E_2 and CG is 9.14 which is significant at .01 level with df 78. It indicates that mean gain score of E_2 and CG of EVS of class III differ significantly. Further the mean gain score of E_2 is 15.23 which is significantly higher than mean gain score of control group which is 4.60.

It is further seen that 't' value between El and E2 is 4.00 which is significant at .01 level df 78. It indicates that the mean gain score of Eland E2 of EVS of class III differ significantly. Further mean gain score of E2 is 15.23 which is higher than mean gain score of El which is 9.80.

Significance of mean difference on pre-test scores of various groups on Math and EVS of class V

From Table 8.16, the calculated value of F is 10.54 of pre-test scores of Math of class V. This value of F is less than the table value at .05 level. It indicates that pre-test scores of all the three groups - E_1, E_2 and CG do not differ significantly. Similarly the calculated value of F is 2.42 is of pre-test scores of Math of class V. This value of F is less than the table value at .05 level. It indicates that pre-test scores of all the three groups do not differ significantly.

Table 8.16
Summary of ANOVA of Pre-test, Post-test and Gain Scores of Math and EVS of Class V

Subject	Stage		Sum of Squares	df	Mean	F	Sig.
Mathematics	Pre-test	Between Groups	36.617	2	18.308	1.540	.219
		Within Groups	1390.850	117	11.888		
		Total	1427.467	119			
	Post-test	Between Groups	160.117	2	80.058	5.581	.005
		Within Groups	1678.475	117	14.346		
		Total	991.125	119			
	Gain	Between Groups	236.600	2	118.300	18.344	.000
		Within Groups	754.525	117	6.449		
		Total	991.125	119			
EVS	Pre-test	Between Groups	247.217	2	123.608	2.420	.093
		Within Groups	5977.150	117	51.087		
		Total	6224.367	119			
	Post-test	Between Groups	2137.217	2	1068.608		
		Within Groups	8090.775	117	69.152		
		Total	10227.992	119			
	Gain	Between Groups	1251.150	2	625.575	31.973	.000
		Within Groups	2289.175	117	19.566		
		Total	3540.325	119			

From Table 8.16, the calculated value of F is 4.48 of post-test scores of Math of class V. The F value is higher than the table value of F at .01 level. It indicates that post-test scores of all groups - E_1, E_2 and CG differ significantly.

It is further seen that F is 15.45 of post-test scores of EVS of class V. The F value is higher than the table value of F at .01 level. It indicates that post-test scores of all groups - E_1, E_2 and CG differ significantly.

From Table 8.16, the calculated value of F is 19.34 of post-test gain scores of Math of class V. The F value is higher than the table value of F at .01 level. It indicates that all post-test gain scores of all groups differ significantly. Similarly it is seen that calculated value of F is 31.97 of post- test gain scores of EVS of class V. The F value is higher than the table value of F. at .01 level. It indicates that all post-test gain scores of all groups differ significantly.

The 't' Values of Significance of Mean Gain Scores Between Three Groups on Math of Class V

Table 8.17 shows that 't' value is 4.40 which is significant at .01 level with df 78. It indicates that the mean gain score of El and CO of Math of class V differ significantly.

Further mean gain score of El is 4.18 that is significantly higher than mean gain score of control group which is 3.03.

Table 8.17

Mean, SD and et' Values of Mean Gain Difference between Various Groups in Math of Class V

		Group	M	SD	N	t-value	Remark
Math	Gain score	E_1	5.18	3.17	40	4.40	Significant at 0.01 level
		Control Group	3.03	1.48	40		
		E_2	6.43	2.67	40	9.14	Significant at 0.01 level
		Control Group	3.03	1.48	40		
		E_1	5.18	3.17	40	1.99	Significant at 0.01 level
		E_2	6.43	2.67	40		

The table also shows that 't' value between E_2 and CO is 6.15 which is significant at .01 level with df 78. It indicates that mean gain score of E_2 and CO of Math of class V differ significantly. Further the mean gain score of E_2 is 6.43 which is significantly higher than mean gain score of control group which is 3.03.

It is further seen tht 't' value between E_1 and E_2 is 1.99 which is significant at .05 level with df 78. It indicates that the mean gain score of $E_1$and E_2 of Math of class V differ significantly. Further mean gain score of E_2 is 6.43 which is higher than mean gain score of E_1 which is 5.18.

't' Values of Significance of Mean Gain Scores between Three Groups on EVS of Class V

Table 8.18 shows that 't' value is 6.04 which is significant at .01 level with df 78. It indicates that the mean gain score of El and CG of EVS of class V differ significantly. Further, mean gain score of El is 11.38 which is higher than mean gain score of control group which is 5.45.

Table 8.18

Mean, SD and et' Values of Mean Gain Difference between Various Groups in EVS of Class V

		Group	M	SD	N	t-value	Remark
EVS	Gain score	E_1	11.38	5.51	40	6.04	Significant at 0.01 level
		Control Group	5.45	2.86	40		
		E_2	12.60	5.42	40	7.39	Significant at 0.01 level
		Control Group	5.45	2.86	40		
		E_1	11.38	5.51	40	4.00	Significant at 0.05 level
		E_2	12.60	5.42	40		

The table further shows that 't' value between E_2 and CG is 12.60 which is significant at .01 level with df 78. It indicates that mean gain score of E_2 and CG of EVS of class V differ significantly. Further the mean gain score of E_2 is 12.62 which is significantly higher than mean gain score of control group with is 5.45.

It is further seen that 't' value between E_1 and E_2 is 2.01 which is significant at .05 level df 78. It indicates that the mean gain score of E_1 and E_2 of EVS of class V differ significantly. Further mean gain score of E_2 is 12.60 which is higher than mean gain score of El which is 11.38.

Teacher Attitude

't' value of significance between pre-test and post-test of the Total Group comprising (E_1 and E_2) of Teachers Attitude towards ETV Programme.

Table 8.19

Mean, SD and et' Values of Pre-test and Post-test Scores of Teacher Attitude towards ETV Programmes

	M	SD	N	t-value	Remarks
Pre-test	142.59	15.67	70	16.55	Significant at 0.01 level
Post-test	156.37	13.76	70		

From table 8.19 it is evident that 't' value is 16.55 that is significant at .01 level with df 69. It indicates that the mean scores of pre-test and post-test differ significantly. Further the mean score of post-test is 156.37 that is significantly higher than the mean score of pre-test which is 142.59. It indicates that teachers attitude towards ETV after the treatment is better than before the treatment.

Learners' Reaction towards ETV Programmes

An interview schedule was used to seek pupils initial reactions towards ETV programme immediately after viewing in the TV class. It was found that most of the pupils like the programmes under 'Tarang' and take interest in viewing. However, they preferred more the enrichment programmes on narration format. They also enjoyed programmes based on dramatization format. Some students of class V expressed that more curriculum based programmes should be shown to them. They were satisfied with the quality of the presentation of programme but unhappy whenever there was disruption due to electricity failure.

In general, the pupils of class III and V expressed that they learned more with understanding certain topics with the help of ETV in the school.

Summary Findings

On the basis of the ANOVA results, the main findings of the experimental study are presented below.

- Pre-test scores of all the three groups - E_1, E_2 and Control Group do not differ significantly for both the subjects - Math and EVS and for both classes III and V do not differ significantly (Table 8.13, 8.16). Hence the groups are considered equivalent at the pre-test stage of the experiment.
- All the post-test gain scores of all the groups differ significantly for both the subjects and for both the classes.
- Mean gain score of E_1 is significantly higher than mean gain score of control group of both the subjects for both the classes.
- Mean gain score of E_2 is significantly higher than mean gain score of control group of both the subjects for both the classes.
- Mean gain score of E_2 is significantly higher than mean gain score of E_1 of both the subjects for both the classes.
- Teacher attitude mean scores of pre-test differ significantly from the mean post-test scores.
- Overall learners' reactions are favourable with regard to interest, learning and quality of programes.

Findings, Implications and Recommendations

Introduction

In this Chapter, first the summary of the study will be presented. It will be followed by discussion of the results in the light of hypotheses of the study and substantiated by the findings of related studies in order to seek a broader perspective on these findings. It is only after testing the individual hypothesis that valid conclusions can be drawn. The findings and conclusions have led the researcher to suggest implications of the study for the learners, teachers, Principals/Headmaster administrators and producers of ETV programmes and also to recommend areas for further research.

Summary

The need of ETV programmes may be essential to tide over the shortcomings of the conventional method. A good medium is an important factor in education. If education is to win in the race, all available resources of the world will need to be mobilized to accept the challenges of science and technology and thus, create a better world. Good education is extremely important for the survival and improvement of democracy in the world. Thus, effective educational programmes through television may help in this regards. But what really makes ETV effective still remains an open question.

In the context of EFA or universal primary education, the effectiveness of ETV programme is primarily related to the students' achievement in Mathematics and General Science, besides language proficiency. In this era, however, when the technology is leaping to its great height, the role of mathematics and science takes the central stage. In order to boost scientific temper among students at this stage of their development and to encourage them to pursue the path of reflective work their achievement in mathematics and science is considered to be of vital importance. Hence, this study to analyze and evaluate the impact of electronic media, particularly, ETV on successfully achieving the goal of universal primary education.

Need of the Study

In the face of educational television and software technology becoming important day by day, television sets are being increasingly installed in schools all over the country, with educational television centres telecasting programmes on various subjects and topics crucial to the course content as well as to the preparation for life, in general. The focus of the study is thus concerned with the impact of educational telecast on primary school students especially in relation to their achievement in mathematics and science. It is aimed at throwing light on the popularity and effectiveness of the television lesson on personality development of the primary school children In Delhi, especially in terms of their achievement and attitude vis-a-vis ETV programmes.

Research Gap

So far limited efforts have been made in India to highlights these issues especially in the context of ETV in primary education in rural and urban areas. There have been a few studies conducted on SIET project by Agarwal (1978), Mohantyand Giri (1977), Mody (1978), Rahman (1977), Shukla and Kumar (1977) and Mohanty & Mohanty (1984) with focus on coverage of ETV programmes at target group level as well as impact of different types of educational programmes in viewers behaviour. On school level ETV there have been studied on utilisation of programmes like Piagnkar (1978), CIET (1984), Goel (1984), Singh and U mare (1986) with concentration of area coverage of schools, time-table attendance of learners regularity in use, etc. There are a number of studies which explore opinion of viewer students as well as teachers on the quality of ETV programmes at school stage such as Shah (1972), EIET (1984b), Goel (1984), Jaiswal (1988), Mohanty & Mohanty (1989), Suriakant and Meenakshi (1989), Sainathambi (1990). Moreover, experiments have been conducted on effectiveness of one way communication mode of ETV on different sample groups of learners, with achievement as major criteria of achievement. They have not explored that affect appropriate strategies for integration of ETV programmes in school activities as well as effectiveness of ETV. This study concentrates on exploring such factors as well as studying comparative effectiveness of ETV and traditional mode.

Rationale of the Study

In recent years, television is being utilized increasingly by developed as well as developing countries to meet the growing demand for education and to improve and enrich instruction. In India, television entered into the field of education in 1959, but it started systematic telecasting of educational programmes at school level after the successful launching of INSAT-1B in 1983.

As highlighted above, ETV has occupied a major place in modern educational technology. Several issues can be raised in the context of ETV at school stage, that - that are the factors that come on the way of use of ETV at primary school stage? It is high time to see that factors affecting effectiveness, efficiency and utilization of ETV in terms of achievement goals in general and instructional objective in specific. It is essential for school teachers to consider:

1. Why they should use television for certain areas of curriculum;

2. "Whether the series and programmes intended for use fit in with the curriculum policies of the school; and
3. How the viewing session will be incorporated with day to day teaching learning activities of schools.

Since primary education system is decentralized in the country questions are to be answered through empirical studies conducted in the country. Whether the user learners benefit from ETV in the context of appreciation of new technology in general and development of positive attitude towards ETV in specific will indicate another dimension of effectiveness of ETV.

The success of ETV will depend upon internal quality of programmes, i.e. language content relevance, visuals, audio, synchronization of audio-video, etc. Scrutiny of these aspects of ETV programme-wise by the participants as well as teacher will be useful in developing totalistic picture about effectiveness of ETV.

As known in general ETV is a modern technology. This is also hypothesized that those who have better acquaintance with new technologies like Radio, TV and Computer may find it flexible to participate in the process of learning through ETV which may lead to better learning outcomes than their non or less technology acquaintance counterparts.

Significance

This study has been undertaken with a view to providing valuable suggestions for planning and organisation of the school television system in general and effective utilisation of educational television programmes for primary classes in particular. The findings of the study will help in effective planning, production, utilisation and evaluation of educational television programmes at the primary stage.

Statement of the Problem

The problem for research may be stated in specific terms as follows:

"A STUDY OF UTILISATION AND EFFECTIVENESS OF EDUCATIONAL TELEVISION (ETV) PROGRAMMES AT PRIMARY SCHOOL LEVEL"

Objectives

Keeping In View the above-stated problem, the main objectives of the study are stated as follows:

1. To conduct a survey of the facilities for utilisation of ETV programmes in Delhi at primary school level.
2. To study the effect of ETV programmes on primary school children - class III and V in terms of their achievement of ETV lessons (EVS and Mathematics) and reaction towards ETV programmes.
3. To study the effect of intervention programmes - post- telecast discussion to be conducted by teachers along with ETV Programmes in primary school children in terms of their achievement of ETV lessons (EVS and Mathematics) and reaction towards ETV programmes.
4. To study the attitude of class teachers towards the quality of ETV programmes.
5. To make recommendations to administrators and producers on different aspects of ETV Programmes.

Hypotheses

The following directional hypotheses are formulated keeping in view the objectives of the study:

1. Learners will utilize ETV programmes to great extent in Delhi at primary classes III and V.
2. Learners exposed to ETV programmes in schools will have higher academic achievement than those who are not exposed to such programmes.
3. Learners exposed to ETV programmes in schools will show more favourable reaction towards ETV than those who are not exposed to such programmes.

4. Learners exposed to ETV programmes in schools along with intervention programmes will have higher academic achievement than those who are exposed to ETV programmes without intervention.
5. Learners exposed to ETV programmes In schools along with intervention programmes will show more favourable reaction towards ETV than those who are exposed to ETV programmes without interventions.
6. Teachers will show more favourable attitude towards ETV programmes after the interventions.

Method

The present study was conducted in two phases - first comprises the status study of utilization of ETV facilities in primary schools; second aimed at investigation into the effectiveness of the ETV programmes broadcast by Doordarshan. Therefore, the normative survey method was employed in the first phase and the experimental method in the second phase.

Design

In the present study, pre-test post-test control design was employed in the experiment which was to be conducted in schools without disturbing the school schedule. Therefore quasi-experimental research design was used. This design provides control of when and to whom the measurement is to arrange a situation in which the effects of variables can be investigated. Control eliminates the differential effects of all variables extraneous to the purpose of the study. The three groups (two experimental) and (a control) are naturally assembled groups as intact classes, which may be similar the subjects are not matched on previous learning achievement of knowledge about ETV lessons in Math and ETV students for grade three and five of primary stage but equated (in mean and standard deviation) with respect to intelligence.

The design comprises one Experiment Group (E_1) which was taught through ETV lessons while the other Experimental Group (E_2) taught ETV lessons followed by teacher discussion.

This treatment continued for about six weeks. Simultaneously the Control Group (CG) was taught by the class teacher. All the three groups were given post-test in Math and EVS (SC and SS) to class III students. Same design was used in case of class V students who were also taught Math and EVS (SC and SS).

Sample

In fact, it was found practically difficult to select schools strictly based on stratified sampling procedure. Therefore, investigator resorted to purposive sampling. The final sample selected for the study is presented in table 9.1.

Table 9.1

Sample of Primary Schools from South District of Delhi

Sl.No.	Type of Management	No. of Primary Schools	Delhi Zone
1.	M.C.D. Primary Schools	30	South
2.	K.V. Primary Sections	4	South
3.	Primary Sections of Sarvodaya Vidyalayas under Directorate of Education	6	South
	Total	40	

Tools

The investigator developed the following tools specifically for collecting required data of this study:

1. Questionnaire for Headmasters and Teachers

A questionnaire was developed to study the nature and extent of utilization of Educational Television Programmes in Delhi schools. It has two sections. Section A on identification of data comprised 20 items while Section B on provision of facilities, knowledge about ETV programme nature and schedule and extent of utilization process of ETV programme comprised 23 main questions and sub-questions of some of the main questions. All answers and information required can be directly fed into the computer for analysis of the data.

2. Achievement Test for Class HI in EVS and Mathematics

The objective was to assess 3rd class students learning achievement in EVS and Math. The achievement test in EVS consisted of 48 multiple choice questions in Science and 30 questions m Social Studies. The achievement test in Mathematics comprised of 27 questions of multiple choice type.

3. Achievement Tests for Class V in EVS and Mathematics

The purpose was to evaluate 5th class students of learning achievement in EVS (Science + Social Studies) and Mathematics. The test consisted of 50 multiple choice questions in Science, 26 questions in Social Studies and 40 questions in Mathematics.

4. Teacher Attitude towards Educational Television (ETV) Programmes - A Rating Scale

The purpose of this scale is to assess teachers' attitude towards ETV programme. The scale consisted of 40 statements to be rated on a Likert type five-point scale.

5. Learner Reactions towards ETV Programmes - An Interview Schedule

Findings

This section presents major findings of the study in two parts. Part I comprises findings of the survey conducted and Part II findings of the experimental study.

Part I: Survey Findings

Availability of ETV Facilities: As many as 22 (73%)MCD schools are having TV sets, 3 (75%) in KVS schools and 2 (33%) in DOE schools. The functional status of TV sets is better in MCD schools and Kendriya Vidyalayas than in schools under Directorate of Education.

Viewing Conditions: It is found that 9 (%) MCD schools are having satisfactory viewing conditions while 2 Kendriya Vidyalayas and none DOE schools having satisfactory viewing conditions. Most of the schools suggested that television viewing place should be separate and a trained teacher should look after the ETV programme.

Knowledge about the Programme and Channel of ETV: It was found that 21 (%) MCD schools, all the Kendriya Vidyalayas and two (33%) DOE schools are aware that national channel (DD1) telecast the ETV programmes. Kendriya Vidyalayas and DOE schools are not aware of Gyan Darshan channel. Majority of schools know about ETV programmes through their Education Officers and some through newspapers.

Purpose of ETV: Majority of schools are using TV sets for viewing ETV programmes, news and sports. Almost 50% students view ETV programmes in the presence of their teachers. However, teachers should actively participate in pre- and post-telecast sessions.

Gyan Darshan Channel: It was found that 50% MCD schools, 100% KVS schools are having separate period for ETV. In the remaining schools there is no fixed period of ETV in the class time-table.

There is a language problem with regard to ETV programmes because in KVS schools textbooks of science and math are in English where as the ETV programme is telecast in Hindi.

Regarding suitability of ETV programmes for particular class and age groups, it was found that generally the programmes are telecast according to the schedule and the context of the syllabus.

Effective Utilization and Related Problems: Majority of the schools reported that pre-telecast preparation is conducted properly. However, Headmasters are of the view that there is no need for viewers to be present 5 minutes before the telecast because previous class teacher does not allow the class to go to ETV room.

The visit by Education Officers has been monthly in majority of schools under different types of managements.

Headmasters of all the three types of schools discuss their problems with the Education Officers. They discuss about the school time-table, maintenance of TV sets and programme schedule of ETV programmes. Headmasters of MCD schools and KVS schools were more serious to discuss their problems with higher authorities.

Problems: Problems related to utilization of ETV include: mechanical disorders of TV sets, failure of electricity, lack of teachers' interest, availability of unscheduled programmes, lack of interest of students, not helpful in completing the curriculum, programme telecast cut abruptly. These are common problems of all the three types of schools.

Effects of Discussion: It was found that pre-and post-telecast discussions make the content clear and create interest among the students for viewing ETV. Thus they can achieve better. It motivates them to learn more and more in addition to the syllabus.

Post-telecast discussion affects both the learner and the learning achievement. It makes difficult concepts clear to the students and reinforces students' learning.

There are certain positive effects on viewers learning due to effective utilization of ETV. These include improvement in students' attendance, enrichment of classroom learning, developing critical and creative thinking and developing scientific temper as positive effects of ETV. It also plays an important role in developing positive attitude towards media which plays an important role in developing social values, feeling of cooperation among the students. However, it dies not effect on punctuality and regularity of students.

Suggestions of Headmasters and Teachers: Several valuable suggestions for making effective utilization of ETV programmes in schools were made by headmasters and teachers. These are: fixed place and time table, suitable ETV room, more curriculum based programmes, students' motivation and awareness to be generated, separate channel for ETV programmes to be life oriented, better publicity of programmes, material to be supplied regularly on time, teacher orientation about the utility of ETV and academic support and monitoring by the Education Officers, etc.

Part II: Findings of the Experimental Study

1. Pre-test scars on the two subjects - Math and EVS of both classes III and V do not differ significantly. Hence the groups - El, E2 and Control Group are taken as equivalent.
2. Post-test scores of Math and EVS of class III of El are significantly higher than post-test scores of Control Group.
3. Post-test scores of Math and EVS of class III of E2 are significantly higher than post-test scores of Control Group.
4. Post-test scores of Math and EVS of class V of El are significantly higher than post-test scores of control group.
5. Post-test scores of Math and EVS of class V of E2 are significantly higher than post-test scores of Control Group.
6. Mean gain scores of Math and EVS of class III of El are significantly higher than mean gain score of Control Group.
7. Mean gain score of Math and EVS of class III of E2 are significantly higher than mean gain score of Control Group.
8. Mean gain scores of Math and EVS of class V of El are significantly higher than mean gain score of Control Group.
9. Mean gain scores of Math and EVS of class V of E2 are significantly higher than mean gain score of the Control Group.

10. Mean gain score of Math and EVS of class V of E2 are significantly higher than mean gin score of the El group.
11. Teacher attitude towards ETV programmes is more favourable than their existing attitude at the pre-test stage.
12. Learner reaction towards ETV programmes is more favourable after viewing the TV programmes in school.

Educational Implications

1. Teacher's interest and motivation in ETV programmes need to be enhanced in order to make the television programmes effective in improving the classroom teaching-learning/process. Therefore, the school system must improve the infrastructural facilities for provision of television sets in functional condition throughout. There is need to have a mechanism which would ensure functionality of TV sets. Principals/Headmasters may be provided with contingent expenditure to meet expenses on immediate repair of any kind of fault in getting the telecast programme viewed by children.
2. There is also a need to establish a Cell for monitoring ETV use in the different schools under different system - MCD, KVS and DOE, etc. The personnel of the Cell should also be competent to guide school teachers in effective instructional use of ETV programmes.
3. There should be regular training of teachers in using ETV programme for curricular purposes. Unless teachers see relevance of the ETV programmes to the content and process of their respective subjects, it cannot be effective and would not serve useful purpose.
4. The producers of the TV programme, e.g., CIET, SIETs, Doordarshan, etc. have to see that

programmes are designed and produced which are curriculum-based. This would help teachers and students motivated to view the programmes.

5. Edusat has recently been launched by Central Government which would be used for 24 hour exclusively for educational purposes. Edusat can be used for more time allocation likely to school telecast. There has to be emphasis both on quality and quantity of instructional programmes for the school stage specially for primary classes.
6. There is need to produce qualitatively superior programmes for instructional purposes. While instructional television may change some of the things the classroom teacher does, the major change will be in the direction of freeing a teacher for more productive use of his time, e.g., working with individuals rather than restricting him.
7. The basic question is not simply how to use television along, but rather how to combine it most effectively with other learning experiences and resources. There are some way of using television which make for better learning than others; some ways of putting school materials on television which result in better teaching than others; some ways of combining television with other learning experiences in school that are more effective than others.
8. There is need to make pre-telecast preparation and post- telecast discussion by the concerned teacher for more effective and purposeful activity. In this context, orientation of ETV teachers becomes not only desirable but essential activity on the part of educational administrators and managers.
9. The well planned ETV programme can motivate students, guide and sharpen their reading relevant materials by providing background and

demonstrations, encourage responsibility for independent learning, arouse curiosity and develop new in sights and the excitement of discovery. Therefore the Principal/Headmaster must take interest in making ETV a well planned activity. Regular meetings with the concerned teachers may be held to ensure that planning and execution of effective utilisation takes place.

This would ensure enhancement of quality teaching due to regular television inputs. Recommendations for Further Research On the basis of the results of this study and investigators experience of field work, the following researches and studies are suggested for further research work in this area.

1. Studies related to impact of educational television on learning outcomes of learners in different school subjects at various levels of schools should be undertaken.
2. The ETV programmes contribute to the academic growth of teachers of primary and elementary classes. It is therefore desirable to undertake research on Teacher learning related to professional development and attitudinal change, etc. due to educational television programmes.
3. Television viewing affects the children's studies at school and home and consequently their performance in school examination. A study on viewing of ETV programmes and its effect on study habits of children and their learning achievement may be undertaken.
4. Mechanism of monitoring and evaluation process goes a long way in making ETV programme effective. It has been suggested that such a mechanism may be planned and implemented by the school systems at the apex level. A study may also be undertaken to see the impact of this mechanism on ETV programme effectiveness.

5. Agencies of programme production for school television should plan design and carry out follow up studies on reactions of teachers and students on their specific programmes telecast for instructional purposes. The feedback may be gainfully utilized for modification of the telecast programmes and for production of the need based programmes for school television in near future.

Bibliography

Anderson, K. & Dermis, N.: Television and Children: Priorities for Research. Report of a Conference at Reston, Virginia, November 5-7, 1975, New York: Federal Foundation (1975).

Anuradha, K.: Children's Television Viewing Behaviour and its Effect on Personal and Educational Development. M.Phil Dissertation, Sri Venkateswara University (1991).

Arnove, R.F. (FD): Educational Television: A Policy Critique and Guide for Developing Countries. New York: Praeger Publishers (1976).

Arularam, I.: Evaluation of the UGC Countrywide Educational Television. M.Phil Dissertation, Madurai Kamaraj University (1990).

Bates, Toney: Formative Evaluation of Educational Television (ed.). Centre for Educational Technology, U.K. (1978).

Behra, S.C.: An Investigation into the Impact of ETV Programmes on the Competency of Teachers of Elementary Schools. Ph.D. Thesis, Utkal University (1990).

Behra, S.C.: Educational Television Programmes. Deep & Deep Publication (1991).

Bhushan, C. (ed.): Broad Educational Objectives and Corresponding ETV Programme Series/Titles for INSAT Transmission (1984085). New Delhi: ETV Unit, CIET, NCERT (1985).

Bogatz, G.A. & Balls, S.: The Second Year of "Sesame Street": A Continuing Education. Princeton, New Jersey: Educational Tesing Service (1971).

Bourret, P.: Television in Rural Areas: A Low-cost Alternative. In R. Arnove (ed.) Educational Television: A Policy Guide and Critique for Developing Countries. Stanford University, School of Education (1973).

Brown, J.W.; Lewis, R.B. & Harcleroad, F.F.: AV Instruction: Materials and Methods (2nd Edn.). New York: McGraw Hill Book Company (1964).

Buch, M.B. (ed.): Fourth Survey of Research in Education. New Delhi: NCERT (1992).

Buch, M.B. (ed.): Fifth Survey of Research in Education. New Delhi, NCERT (1983-1988).

Borton, T.: Dual Audio Television. Harvard Educational Review, Butman, R.C.: Satellite Television for India: Teacher-Economic Factors. Cambridge, Mass: MIT (1972).

Chakrabarti, S.K.: Audio-Visual Education in India. Calcutta and New Delhi: Oxford Book Company (1967).

Chau, G.C. & Schramm, W.: Learning from Television: What the Research Says. Stanford: Stanford University, Institute of Communication Research (1967).

Chaudhary, S. Sohanvir: Teachers' Attitude towards Television (STV) and its Relationship to Mass Media Behaviour and Job Satisfaction. Ph.D. Thesis, University of Delhi (1990).

Childers, P. & Ross, K.: The Relationship between Television and Students' Achievement. Journal of Educational Research, 66, pp. 317-319 (1983).

Choat, E.H. Griffin & Hobert, D.: Educational TV and the Curriculum for Children upto the Age of Seven Years. British Journal of Educational Technology, Vol. 17(3), London: Council of Educational Technology, October (1986).

Chu, G.C. & Schramm, W.: Learning from Television: What the Research says. Washington D.C.: National Association of Educational Broadcasting (1967).

CIET: A Study of the Impact of the ETV programmes on the Children of Classes IV-V in Sambalpur District (Orissa). Mimeographed, New Delhi: NCERT (1983).

Clark, W.J.: Of Children and Television. Cincinnati Oh: Xavier University (1951).

Corteen, R.S.: Television and Reading Skills. In Williams, T.M. (ed.) The Impact of Television: A Natural Experiment involving Three Communities, Symposium Presented at Meeting of the Canadian Psychological Association, Vancouver, B.C. June (1977).

Dean, T. Jamison; Steven J. Klees & Stuart J. Wells: The Cost of Educational Media. Sage Publication (1978).

Dorr, A.; Granes, S.B. & Philips, E.: Television Literacy for Young Children. Journal of Communications, 30: 17-83 (1980).

Dunham, Franklin: Television in our Schools. Bulletin, No. 16 (1952). Encyclopedia of Educational Research (Vol. 2). London: McMillan Co. Collier, McMillan Ltd. (Fourth Edition) (1969).

Evans, S. & Oklees, S.: ETV Program Production in the Ivory Coast. Washington D.C.: Academy for Educational Development (1972).

Friedrich, L.K. & Stein, A.H.: Prosocial Television and Young Children: The Effects of Verballabeling and Role-playing on Learning and Behaviour. Child Development, 46: 27-38 (1975).

Furu, T.: Television and Children's life: A before-after Study. Japan Broadcasting Corporation (NHK) (1960).

Furu, T.: The Functions of Television for Children and Adolescents. Tokyo: Sophia University Press (1971).

Gadberry and Schneider: Effects of Parental Restrictions on TV-Viewing.

Garrett, H.E.: Statistics in Psychology and Education. Bombay: Vakils, Faffer and Simons Ltd. (1979).

Gene, R. Hawls; Lynne Salop Hawls: The Concise Dictionary of Education: A Hudson Group Book. New York: Van Nost Rand Reinhold Company.

Ghosh, Sunanda; Educational Reporting on TV in Tamil Nadu. Indian Educational Review, Vol. 27 (2), pp. 110-115, (1992).

Goel, D.R.: Educational Television in India; Organization and Utilization. Baroda: CASE, MSU (1984).

Goel, D.R.: INDO-US Sub Commission Project Classroom 2000. University News, New Delhi: AIU, Vol. XXXI, No. 49, December 6 (1993).

Goel, D.R.; Jaiswal, K.: ISRO-UGC Talk-Back Experiment in India. University News, New Delhi: AIU, January (1992).

Grattan, Donald: Television in Education. Journal of APLET, Vol. X, No. 3, May (1973).

Greenfield, P.: Radio and Television Experimentally Compared: Effects of the Medium on Imagination and Transmission of Content. Final Report to National Institute of Education, Teaching and Learning Program, 1982. in Beagles-Roos, J. & Gat, 1., Specific Impact of Radio and Television on Children's Story Comprehension, Journal of Educational Psychology, 75, pp. 128-137 (1983).

Greenhilf, L.P.: Penu State Experiment with Two-way Audio System for CCTV. NAF Journals, 23, pp. 73-78 (1964).

Greenstein, J.: Effects of Television upon Elementary School Grades. Journal of Education Research, 48, pp. 161-576 (1959).

Himmelweit, H.T.; Oppenheim, A.N. & Vince, P.: Television and the Child: An Empirical Study of Effect of Television on the Young. London: Oxford University Press (1958).

Himmelweit. H.: Youth, Television and Experimentation. In Cultural Role of Broadcasting, Tokyo: Horo Bunka Foundation (1978). Huston and Wright: Children's Processing of Television.

Jaiswal, K.: A Study of Higher Education Science Education Television Programmes in Terms of their Contents, Presentation, Students; Creations and Effectiveness. Ph.D. Thesis, Devi Ahilya Vishvavidyalaya (1992).

Jamison, D. & KItes, S.: The Cost of Instructional Radio and Television for Developing Countries. Instructional Sciences, 4, pp. 333-387 (1975).

Joint Council of Educational Television: Four Years of Progress in Educational Television. Washington: p. 18 (1956).

Joshi, V.: A Study of the Effectiveness of School Television Programmes in Science at the Secondary School Level. Ph.D. Thesis, The Maharaja Sayajirao University of Baroda (1987).

Kornadt and Abankova: Programmed Learning and Educational Technology. In Gerhard Tulodziecki (ed.) Educational Television in Federal Republic of Germany, Vol. 14, No. 2. May (1977).

Koul, B.N. (ed.): Non-Print Instructional Media: The Television. New Delhi: Indira Gandhi National Open Unviersity (1987).

Lefrane, R.: Educational Television in Nigeria. In W. Schramm, *et.al*. (ed.), New Educational Media in Action: Core Studies for Planners, Vol. Il, Paris: UNESCO International Institute for Educational Planning (1967).

Lesser, G.S.: Children and Television: Lessons from Sesame Sheet. New York: Random House (1974).

Libert, R.M.; Neale, J.M. & Davichon, E.S.: The Early Window: Effects of Television on Children and Youth. New York: Programon (1973).

Logan, B. (ed.): Television Awareness Training. New York: Media Action Research Center (1977).

Lyle, J. Colombia's National Programme for Primary Level Television Instruction. In W. Schramm, *et.al*. (ed.), New Educational Media in Action: Core Studies for Planners, Vol. II, Paris: UNESCO Institute for Educational Planning (1967).

Maccoby, E.E.: Television: Its Impact on School Children. Public Opinion Quarterly, 444 (1951).

MacLean, R.: Television in Education. London: Methuen Education (1968).

Madden, J.V.: Experimental Study of Student Achievement in Relation to Class Size. School Science and Mathematics (1968).

Masterman: Teaching about Television. London: Macmillan (1980).

Mayo, J.K.: Hornik, R.C. & Mc Anany, E.G.: Educational Reforms with Television: The El Salvador Experience. Stanford: University Press (1976).

Medley, D.M. & Mitzel, H.E.: Measuring Classroom Behaviour by Systematic Observation. In Gage, N.L. (ed.) Handbook of Research on Teaching, Chicago: Rand McNally (1963).

Melody, W.: Children's Television: The Economics of Exploitation. New Hanen: Yole University Press (1978).

MHRD: National Policy on Educaton-1986. New Delhi: Department of Education, Ministry of Human Resource Development (1986).

Miles, J.R.: Asking the Right ETV Research Questions. Educational Broadcasting Review, December (1968).

Ministry of Education and Culture: Report of the Study Group on INSAT Television Utilisation for Education and Development. New Delhi: MOE, Government of India (1981).

Mohanty, J. & Giri, A.P.: A Study on School Board Chat Programmes. Directorate of Higher Education. Orissa (1977).

Mohanty, J. & Mohanty, P.C.: A Study of the Impact of SITE on Attendance and Enrolment in Primary School. Orissa: SCERT.

Mohanty, J.: A Study of ETV Programmes under SITE. Studies on Educational Television and Radio Programmes, Bhubaneswar: Educational Technology Cell, Directorate of Higher Education, Orissa (1976).

Mohanty, J.; Giri, A.P. & Mohanty, P.C.: A Study of ETV Programmes during the in-service Teachers Training Course. Studies on Educational Television and Radio Programmes, Bhubaneswar: ET Cell, Directorate of Education, Orissa (1976).

Mohanty, P.C.: A Critical Study of the Educational Television Programmes for Primary School Children in the State of Orissa. Ph.D. Thesis, Utkal University (1986).

Moir, Guthrie: Teaching and Television: ETV Explained. London: Pergamon Press (1967).

Morgan, M. & Gross, L.: Television and Educational Achievement and Aspiration. In Pearl, Bouthilet & Lazard, Calif, August (1983).

NCERT: Krishi Darshan, Agricultural Television Project: Continuous Evaluation. Report-I, New Delhi: Department of Adult Education (1969).

NCERT: A Report on ETV Utilisation in Orissa. Mimeographed, New Delhi: NCERT (1983-84).

NCERT: History and Development of ETV in India: A Report. Mimeographed, New Delhi: NCERT (1984).

Neurath, P.: School Television in Delhi. New Delhi: All India Radio (1966).

Palmon Aimee Dorr: Children and the Faces of Television. Brace Jovanovica Publication (1980).

Patricia Marks Greenfield: Mind and Media: The Effects of Television, Video Games and Computers. Cambridge, Massachusetts: Harvard University Press (1984).

Peter Jarvis; Routiledcre: An International Dictionary of Adult and Continuing Education. London and New York Publication (1990).

Pezdek and Lehrer: The Relationship between Reading and Cognitive Processing of Media. Pezdek, K. and Stevesn, E., Children's Memory for Auditory and Visual Information on Television, Developmental Psychology, forthcoming.

Phi Delta Kuppa Carter V. Good (ed]: Dictionary of Education. New York/London: McGraw Hill Book Company Inc (1945).

Phutela, R.L.: A Pilot Projection interactive Video Technology in the Orientation Programme of Primary School Teachers. New Delhi: CIET, NCERT Project (1996).

Phutela, R.L.: A Study on the Effects of Comics and Comic Television Serials on Children. Fifth Survey of Research in Education, New Delhi: NCERT (1991).

Potter, R.L.: TV and My Classroom: An Evolutionary Tale. Television and Children, 2, pp. 19-20 (1979).

Rahman, S.: Satellite Instructional Television Experiment - A Study in Educational Television. (Udaya-Bhanu), New Delhi: Ministry of Education and Social Welfare, Government of India (1977).

Sahoo, N.: Effectiveness of Countrywide Classroom ETV Programmes in Social Sciences with and without Talk Back mode. Ph.D. Thesis, Indore: DAVV (1994).

Sahoo, N.: Effectiveness of Educational Television Programmes of CIET for Teacher Education.

Sahoo, Namita & Goel, D.R.: Effectiveness of CWeR in Different Institutions through different modes. Journal of Research in Educational Media, 2(2), New Delhi (1995).

Sahoo, Namita: A Study of UGC Countrywide Classroom ETV Programmes in terms of their Contents, Presentation and Effectiveness with and without talkback. M.Ed. Dissertation, Indore: IOE, DAVV (1991).

Sahoo, Namita: Effectiveness of Countrywide Classroom ETV Programmes in Social Sciences with and without talkback and through Simulated Interactive Mode. Ph.D. thesis, Indore: DAVV (1994).

Sahoo, P.K. & Mallick: Study on Attitude of Rural Primary School Children towards ETV. Abstract of Educational Technology, Vol. I (1993).

Sahoo, P.K.: Open Learning System. New Delhi: Uppal (1994).

Sarangi, Dlbakar: A Study of IGNOU ETV Programmes in terms of their Effectiveness through Direct, Simulated Talkback and Interactive Modes. M.Phil Dissertation, Indore: IOE, DAVV (1992).

Saxena, G.: Educational TV Programmes. Education Quarterly, Vol. XXXVIII(I), New Delhi: Ministry of Human Resource Development, Spring (1986).

Scarborough, M.L.: The Educational Value of Non-Educational Television: A Study of Children's Response to General Programme Material. London: Independent Broadcasting Authority (1973).

SCERT: ETV Utilisation in Orissa: A Report. Mimeographed, January (1986).

Schramm, W.; Lyle, J.; & Parkar, E.B.: Television in the Lines of our Children. Stanford: Stanford University of Hawaii (1972).

Scott, L.F.: Television and School Achievement. Phi. Delta Kappan, 38, pp. 25-58 (1956).

Seth: A Study on the impact of ETV Programmes with and without Teacher's Intervention on Primary School Children in Delhi. Fourth Survey of Research in Education, New Delhi: NCERT (1983).

Seth, Indu: A Study of the Effectiveness of Educational Television on the Educational Development of Primary Children. Ph.D. Thesis, Baroda: CASE, M.S. University of Baroda (1983).

Shah, M.C.: The Scope, Utility and Limitations of Educational Television in India. Ph.D. Thesis, Baroda: M.S. University of Baroda (1972).

Singh, B.B.: Effectiveness of UGC Countrywide Classroom Programmes on Models of Teaching with and without talkback and Through Interactive Mode. M.Phil Dissertation, Indore: IOE, DAVV (1991).

Singh, J.: A Report on ETV Utilisation with special reference to TV maintenance in Sambalpur (INSAT Evaluation Series-2). Mimeographed, New Delhi: CIET, NCERT (1983).

Singh, J. & Singh, A.K.: A Study of the Impact of ET V Programmes on the Children of Classes IV-V in Sambalpur District (Orissa) INSAT Evaluation Series-3, Mimeographed, New Delhi: CIET, NCERT (1983).

Singh, J. & Singh, A.K.: Report of the ETV Utilization in Orissa (Period ending December, 1983). INSAT Evaluaiton Series-4, Mimeographed, New Delhi: CIET, NCERT (1984).

Singh, J.; Prasad, S.; Bajpai, A. & Kaur, R.J.: Pre-telecast Testing of the ETV Programmes: Some Observations (INSAT Evaluation Series-7). Mimeographed, New Delhi: CIET, NCERT (1984).

Singh, J. & Umare, R.S.: A Repot on ETV Utilization in Maharashtra State. New Delhi: Central Institute of Educational Technology, NCERT (1986).

Spaulding, S.: Communication Potential of Pictorial Illustrations. Audio-visual Communication (1956).

Speagle, R.E.: Educational Reform and Instructional Television in El Salvador Cost Benefit and Pay offs. Washington D.C.: Academy for Educational Development (1972).

Stein, A.H. & Friedrich, L.K.: Impact of Television on Children and Youth. In Hetherington, E.M. (ed.) Review of Child Development Research. Vol. V, Chicago: University of Chicago Press (1975).

Stein, A.H. & Fredrick, L.K.: The Impact of Television on Children and Youth. In Hetherington, E.M. (ed.) Review of Child Development Research, Vol. V, Chicago: University of Chicago Press, pp. 183-256 (1975).

Stevemon, H.W.: Television and the Behaviour of Preschool Children. In Murray, J.P.; Rubinstein, E.A. & Comstock, G.A. (ed.) Television and Social Behaviour, Vol. III, Washington D.C.: Supt. of Docs, U.S. Government Print Off (1972).

Sudame, G.R. and Goel, D.R.: Educational Television in India: Organization and Utilization. EPA Bulletin, Vol. 8, Nos. 1 & 2, New Delhi: NIEPA, April & July (1985).

Television for Learning: A Catalog of Reading Programs and Teachers' Guides. Television and Children, 1979, 2, 36-38. A DOIT Leifer, "Teaching with Television and Film" in Gage, N.L. (ed.) Psychology of Teaching Methods, National Society for the Study of Education Yearbook, Chicago: University of Chicago Press (1976).

UNESCO: World Communication: Press Radio, TV and Film. Paris (1964).

Welb, S. & Klees, S.: A Cost Analysis of the Hagerstown ITV system. Journal of Educational Technology System (1976).

Wolgamuth, D.A.: Comparative Study of Three Techniques of Student Research in Television Teaching: The Effectiveness of an Electrical Feedback System. NDEA Title UU Project No. 483,

Washington D.C.: US Office of Education (1961).

Index

A

American Council on education, 9

Analysis and interpretation, 76-105

analysis of data of experimental study, 97-98

educational television programme in schools, 76-77

effective utilization of ETV programme, 85-96

effectiveness of ETV programmes – an experimental study, 96-97

Gyan Darshan Channel, 84-85

introduction, 76

learners reaction towards ETV programmes, 104-105

purposes of ETV, 82-83

significance of mean difference on pre-test scores of various groups on math and EVS of class V, 100-103

status of ETV facilities, 77-82

t values of significance of mean gain scores between three groups on

EVS of class III, 99-100

EVS of class V, 103-104

maths of class III, 98-99

teacher attitude, 104

ANOVA, 33, 96, 105

C

CAI, 45

CEC, 18

Chi Square test, 40

CNIV, 43

Computer Diploma, 40

Control-Experimental Groups, 42

CTM, 46, 48, 49

D

Democracy, 24

DEO, 74

E

Educational television programme in India on south zone Delhi primary schools, 62-75

introduction, 62

statement of the problem, 62

utilization and effectiveness of educational television programmes at primary school level, 63

EFA, 24

ETV, 4, 24, 38

programmes, 60, 63

EVS, 27

F

Federal Communication Commission in USA, 10

Findings, implications and recommendations, 106-120

introduction, 106
need of the study, 107
rationale of the study, 108-109
research gap, 107-108
significance, 109
statement of the problem, 109
Ford Foundation, 15

G

Good education, 24
Gulf War, 13

H

HAU, 51
HODs, 51

I

Introduction, 1-5
flexibility, 4
higher quality of instruction, 4
influence of television on children, 3-5
mass education, 4
reduce dependency on teacher, 4
social equality in education, 4

K

Karnataka, 16
KGKs, 51
KVS, 74

L

Literature related to educational television, 28-61
Akutsu, 29
Behera, 38
Butler, 35
Chaudhary, S. Sohanvir, 33
Criffin, 32
Ghosh, Sunanda, 34
introduction, 28
Jaiswal, K., 39
Mohanty, P.C., 37
observation, 60-61
Ogawa, 34
recent Indian studies on effectiveness of ETV, 40-60
Sahoo, P.K., 39
Saulat Rahman, 29
Seth, 36
Singh and Singh, 31
Singh and Singh, 36
studies on provision and utilization of ETV facilities, 29-34
studies related to impact of ETV programmes, 34-40
Taglides, 30
Torres, 37

M

Major educational television projects, 14-19
Delhi agriculture television project, 15-16
gyan-darshan educational channel (2000), 18-19
IGNOU-doordarshan telecast (1991), 18
Indian national satellite project (INSAT-1982), 17
post-SITE project (1977), 16
UGC-higher education television project (JETV-1984), 17-18
MCD, 74
Midwestern University Campus, 7
MNGI, 46